A MYTH RETOLD

C. S. LEWIS SECONDARY STUDIES SERIES

C. S. Lewis (1898–1963) taught Medieval and Renaissance Language and Literature at Oxford and Cambridge Universities for almost four decades. He wrote much for publication: literary criticism, poetry, theology, spirituality, science fiction, juvenile literature, novels, autobiography, but alas no plays. Over and above that, he kept up a fierce correspondence for decades; 3,228 letters of his compiled and edited by Walter Hooper have been published in three volumes (2000–2006).

Hooper, long the literary adviser to the Estate of C. S. Lewis, has done much of the primal research on Lewis, editing and seeing to publication perhaps a dozen collections of Lewis's shorter writings (essays, articles, addresses; literary criticism; diaries).

Most Lewis books are still in print in one way or another. But various studies of and commentaries on Lewisiana by others have not had the same longevity. Many are now out of print, but there is much research and review yet to be done.

To aid present and future scholars, Wipf and Stock Publishers has established a series devoted to worthy books on or about Lewis. Perhaps because I have done four books on or about Lewis, Wipf and Stock has asked me to be the general editor of the series.

William Griffin
Series Editor for C. S. Lewis Studies 2007

A Myth Retold

Re-encountering C. S. Lewis as Theologian

EDITED BY
Martin Sutherland

WIPF & STOCK · Eugene, Oregon

A MYTH RETOLD
Re-encountering C. S. Lewis as Theologian

C. S. Lewis Secondary Studies Series

Copyright © 2014 Martin Sutherland. All rights reserved. Except for brief quotations in critical publications or reviews, no part of this book may be reproduced in any manner without prior written permission from the publisher. Write: Permissions, Wipf and Stock Publishers, 199 W. 8th Ave., Suite 3, Eugene, OR 97401.

Wipf & Stock
An Imprint of Wipf and Stock Publishers
199 W. 8th Ave., Suite 3
Eugene, OR 97401

www.wipfandstock.com

ISBN 13: 978-1-61097-247-5

Manufactured in the USA.

Contents

Introduction   vii
Martin Sutherland

1   Convergence in Joy: A Comparison of the Devotional Practices of Lewis and That "Dreadful Man Karl Barth"   1
    David W. Williams

2   Corresponding Theologically with C. S. Lewis   24
    Geoffrey Holt

3   Revelation and Natural Theology   38
    Roger Driver-Burgess

4   C. S. Lewis's Argument against Naturalism   57
    John Owens

5   God and the Moral Law in C. S. Lewis   69
    Matthew Flannagan

6   C. S. Lewis, Animals, and Nature Red in Tooth and Claw   93
    Nicola Hoggard Creegan

7   Mere Christianity for Mere Gods: Lewis on Theosis   110
    Myk Habets

8   A Narnian Way to Heaven: Judgment, Universalism, and Hell in Lewis's Vision   130
    Martin Sutherland

Bibliography   145

Introduction

MARTIN SUTHERLAND

EXPLORING THE LEWIS MAP

IN HIS 2004 STUDY *Mere Theology: A Guide to the Thought of C. S. Lewis*,[1] Will Vaus sets out to organise Lewis's ideas along recognisably "theological" themes. It is an attempt to portray the whole of Lewis's thought and to test it by scripture. In other words, to come as close as could be to treating Lewis's theology in a systematic fashion. In the present volume, the various authors join Vaus (and many others in recent Lewis studies) who take Lewis seriously as a theologian. However the approach is very different. This is not a synthetic account of Lewis's theology, representing his *oeuvre* as an integrated continuum. If we were to adopt Lewis's own image of theology as a map we might see Vaus to be refining Lewis's map to a set of directions. In the present volume the authors consider the map as a picture, a depiction of reality, pausing at points in the landscape to consider how it is that Lewis has drawn this or that feature. Admittedly, in a study of C. S. Lewis this approach carries its risks. Lewis himself was wary of those who linger in the map itself and neglect its purpose of drawing them into the life of God. Yet there remains merit in seeking to understand Lewis's cartography better—to discern more keenly the manner in which he marks his map.

David Williams considers Lewis as a devotional theologian. The notion or image of "joy" is a well-known theme in Lewis's writings. Williams finds in this an unexpected connection to the theological method and

1. Vaus, *Mere Theology*.

INTRODUCTION

motivation of Karl Barth—a "real theologian" whom Lewis would associate with much that he found unattractive in dogmatic theology. Both, Williams argues, saw beyond their theology, to beauty. Geoff Holt by contrast enters the Lewis map not through his devotional practice but through his massive correspondence, now made available in the three impressive volumes edited by the indefatigable Walter Hooper. For someone like Lewis, who connected theology inextricably to experience, the immediacy of the letters provides an irreplaceable hermeneutical tool for understanding his intent and meaning.

Three essays do some heavy lifting around Lewis's philosophical method. Roger Driver-Burgess engages with Lewis's use of the natural world. Is this a new form of natural theology? With a focus on three works from the 1940s, *The Abolition of Man*, "Transposition" and *Miracles*, Driver-Burgess finds Lewis to be wrestling with the paradox of the God who is both hidden and revealed. If we are to understand Lewis, Driver-Burgess suggests, we must not seek from him "a balanced and systematic theological, ontological or epistemological exposition." Rather, "he is attempting to persuade." John Owens also engages with *Miracles*, ultimately connecting it to the visceral *A Grief Observed*, from near the end of Lewis's life. Lewis, Owens argues, rejected "naturalism" not merely because it was reductionist but because it fails its own claims by being "incompatible with rational thinking." Owens suggests that the argument runs deeper and further—that naturalism "excludes any real relation to reality." Third in this trilogy of essays is Matthew Flannagan on God and the Moral Law in Lewis. Taking his cue from *Mere Christianity*, Flannagan shows that here too Lewis rejects naturalism, in this case because of the phenomenon of the moral law. But Lewis's theism does not merely derive from an identification of moral obligations with the commands of God. Lewis was not prepared to subsume the moral law into divine command, but in other places reserves for it an independent existence. This raises problems which, Flannagan holds, are not resolved in Lewis's writings. More sophisticated versions of divine command theory are used to restore the most straightforward reading of the argument in *Mere Christianity*.

The final three essays examine aspects of Lewis's theological positions. Nicola Hoggard Creegan brings a new perspective on Lewis's proposals on *The Problem of Pain*. For all Lewis's skill as "a tame animal story teller" he does not, Hoggard Creegan suggests, have a fully developed theology of animals. This is an omission, and one which can be fruitfully engaged by

INTRODUCTION

reconsidering the notion and import of the human "fall" and the possibility of animal salvation in the light of contemporary developments in science.

Salvation is also a theme in the remaining two essays. In "Mere Christianity for Mere Gods," Myk Habets explores the notion of theosis in Lewis and in current debates on this most mysterious of expressions of the Christian hope. Lewis may have espoused a "mere Christianity," but he did not resile from mystery. Indeed he insisted upon it. Habets explores a wide range of Lewis's work to draw out his picture of what it means to "participate in the Divine nature." Martin Sutherland considers similar issues, although he clearly comes into Lewis's map at a different point. Ultimate life, life beyond physical death, is traditionally pictured by such terms as Heaven, Hell, Purgatory etc, supported by concepts like judgment and damnation. Sutherland argues that Lewis recasts these images, especially in his fictional writings. The character of ultimate life is intimately bound up with Lewis's notion of personhood. It is inextricably linked to relationship and the will. Thus, Hell and Heaven are not "real" places of destination, created by God. Hell is in fact non-reality, generated (or perhaps degenerated) by its inhabitants. Heaven by contrast is experience of God himself, a "divinely bestowed glory."

MERE THEOLOGY?

What picture emerges, then, of the way Lewis draws his map? What sort of theologian is he? As Myk Habets notes, Lewis would on occasion eschew any claim to doing "real theology"—"I walk *in mirabilis supra me* [things too wonderful for me]." It is a fine note of humility, but it belies a deeper truth, that Lewis, though not claiming to do what the "real theologians" do, was nonetheless pursuing a sophisticated version of the theological task.

The clue to this is found in Lewis's discussion of his key exemplar: the sixteenth century divine, Richard Hooker (1554–1660). Hooker, Lewis identifies, espouses an interwoven religious vision. In distinction from the sharply drawn (though anachronistically denominated) "Barthianism" of a Calvinist/Puritan view of authority, Hooker rejected the dualistic division between that which is revelation and that which is not—"the theology which set a God of inscrutable will 'over against' the 'accused nature of Man' with all its arts, sciences, traditions, learning and merely human virtues."[2] This "ruthless antithesis" is the framework Lewis himself would

---

2. Lewis, *English Literature*, 453.

INTRODUCTION

be fighting in most of his Christian works. It explains his antipathy to Barth and the "Barthianism" he regards as Hooker's target. Although, on some fronts, as explored in David Williams's essay, Lewis and Barth may be seen to share many commitments, Barth nonetheless represented for Lewis a dangerous tendency in Christian theology. "'Under judgement' is their great expression. They all talk like Covenanters or Old Testament prophets. They don't think Human reason or human conscience of any value at all. . . . Sometimes the results are refreshing. . . . But the total effect is withering."[3]

It is therefore worth considering just what it was in Hooker's alternative to this severe gospel that Lewis identified so positively. Crucially, Hooker's universe was interwoven, rather than divided.

> "All things which are in the Church ought to be of God. But they may be two ways accounted such" (vii. xi. 10). For, often, "the same thing which is of men may also justly and truly be said to be of God" (ibid.). . . . For explicit divine injunction, embodied in scripture, is but "a part of that rule" which we were created to live by (vii. xi. 10). There is another part, no less God-given, which Hooker calls "nature" (Pref. vi. I), "law rational, which men commonly use to call the Law of Nature" (I. viii. 9), "the light of Reason" (viii. 3). The most permanent value of Hooker's work lies in his defence of that light.[4]

Lewis's own "defence of that light" is of course crucial to his thinking. The value and validity of "reason"—understood much more broadly than mere rational process, to mean something like the human capacity to grasp the mysterious—is part of Lewis's own "permanent value." Importantly it suggests a very different vision for theology.

When Lewis rhetorically conceded greater expertise to "real theologians" he no doubt had in mind those who conceived the task of theology very differently from himself. Alistair McGrath has recently pointed out that the Germanic stream of theology, sourced in the nineteenth century, with Schleiermacher at its wellspring, with which Barth contended but of which he was nonetheless a part, has been assumed to represent what "real theologians" do. However, this highly systematised approach risks "theological over-precision, metaphysical inflation and excessive conceptual elaboration" of a type which Lewis abhorred. Lewis's approach is more organic, lived from the inside out, less defined. James Como likens it to

3. Lewis, *Collected Letters II*, 351.
4. Lewis, *English Literature*, 453–54.

INTRODUCTION

quantum theory, in which the movement and the location of the electron are unknowable together and "more vexing still, . . . merely observing the phenomenon changes it."[5] McGrath sounds perhaps a too ethnocentric note when he situates Lewis within "a decidedly English approach to theology, which assumes and explores the interconnectedness of religious experience, thought, writing and life."[6] However this description does resonate with Lewis's appreciation of Hooker.

> God is unspeakably transcendent; but also unspeakably immanent. It is this conviction which enables Hooker, with no anxiety, to resist any inaccurate claim that is made for revelation against reason, Grace against Nature, the spiritual against the secular. . . . Certainly, the Christian revelation is 'that principal truth in comparison whereof all other knowledge is vile'; but only in comparison. All kinds of knowledge, all good arts, sciences, and disciplines come from the father of lights and are 'as so many sparkles resembling the bright fountain from which they rise' (III. viii. 9).

Crucially, "we must not think that we glorify God only in our specifically religious actions. . . . Not, of course, that our different modes of glorifying God are on a level."[7] But, then, that is the point. It is very the diversity and hierarchy of these elements which guarantees their beauty, their truth. We meet on all levels the divine wisdom shining through "the beautiful variety of all things" in their "manifold and yet harmonious dissimilitude" (III.xi.8).[8]

We are forced, thus, to wonder whether synthetic approaches to Lewis such as that of Vaus are perhaps misguided. In his incisive study of Lewis's thought, Paul Holmer points out that Lewis's "discovery is that there is no single and univocal way of being rational; for rationality cannot altogether exclude emotion, it cannot say all myths are prescientific and leave matters at that, it cannot be detached and exclude a life of feelings and pathos."[9] Others have picked up the essential dynamics of Lewis's thought. Como describes *The Pilgrim's Regress* as "a complex eruption wrought tightly of imagination, reason and purpose" which forms Lewis's "rhetorical

---

5. Como, "C. S. Lewis' Quantum Church," 90.
6. McGrath, *Intellectual World*, 167.
7. Lewis, *English Literature*, 460.
8. Ibid., 461.
9. Holmer, *C. S. Lewis*, 99–100.

template."¹⁰ Paul Fiddes sees that in his discussions of trinity, incarnation and life that Lewis is "touching doctrine with the glow of imagination."¹¹ Austen Farrer, Oxford clergyman, philosopher and Lewis confidant, identified this instinctive interweaving.

> It was this feeling intellect, the intellectual imagination which made the strength of his religious writings. Some of those unsympathetic to his convictions saw him as an advocate who bluffed a public eager to be deceived, by the presentation of uncertain arguments as cogent demonstrations. . . . But his real power was not proof, it was depiction. There lived in his writings a Christian universe which could be both thought and felt, in which he was at home, and in which he made his reader at home. Moral issues were presented with sharp lucidity, and related to the divine will; and once so seen, could never again be seen otherwise. We who believe will ask no more. Belief is natural, for the world is so. It is enough to let it be seen so.¹²

As, indeed, some of the essays in this volume point out, Lewis can be questioned at places for the logic or, more exactly, the systematic cogency, of his arguments. His moral stances, his assumptions, his apparent relegation of women, can seem outdated, a little embarrassing even to his modern admirers. But these criticisms fault Lewis on scales he did not claim. Calling for a more subtle appreciation of Hooker, Lewis acknowledged that his great exemplar had his flaws and can easily look outdated. But this is to read Hooker wrong.

"Usually, in past controversies, the premiss which neither side questioned, now seems the shakiest of all. The permanent appeal of a great philosophical work, however, seldom depends entirely on its success in solving the problem which the author had set himself."¹³

The true success of a thinker, that which establishes its "permanent appeal" lies in the fact that "every system offers us a model of the universe; Hooker's model has unsurpassed grace and majesty."¹⁴

It is this "grace and majesty" which matters most about Hooker's thought. The power of the metaphors and analogies is more significant than

---

10. Como, "C. S. Lewis' Quantum Church," 90.
11. Fiddes, "On Theology," 94.
12. Farrer, *The Brink of Mystery*, 46.
13. Lewis, *English Literature*, 459.
14. Ibid.

the precision of their 'truth." In Farrer's words, it is the richness of the images, rather than the exactness of their proofs, which enables the Christian universe to be both thought and felt. In his final major work, Lewis rejects the notion that it is even possible to construct some deeper, more authentic picture of God. In *Letters to Malcolm Chiefly on Prayer* Lewis defends the use of images.

> To talk of "meeting" is, no doubt, anthropomorphic; as if God and I could be face to face, like two fellow creatures, when in reality He is above me and within me and below me and all about me. That is why it must be balanced by all manner of metaphysical and theological abstractions. But never, here or anywhere else, let us think that while anthropomorphic images are a concession to our weakness, the abstractions are the literal truth. Both are equally concessions: each singly misleading, and the two together mutually corrective. Unless you sit to it very lightly, continually murmuring "Not thus, not thus, neither is this Thou," the abstraction is fatal.[15]

The Christian is to embrace the imagery. As Farrer suggests of Lewis, "his real power was not proof, it was depiction." We must understand Lewis's work—all of it: the apologetics, the fiction, the devotional writing, the criticism—as a style of theology—markedly different from the hegemonic, systematic kind—but a genuine style of theology nonetheless. It might properly be called "mere theology," in the true Lewisian sense of that which does not claim more for itself than it properly should. Thus "we must not smuggle in the idea that we can throw the analogy away and, as it were, get in behind it to a purely literal truth."[16] Indeed, "our abstract thinking is itself a tissue of analogies."[17] Systems can of course be beautiful and satisfying, but in doing so they draw attention to themselves and indeed risk becoming the point of their own existence. Lewis's theology is true, but it depicts, rather than proves. By it the true myth is retold, by it the universe is re-read, by it we are reminded of "the beautiful variety of all things."[18]

---

15. Lewis, *Letters to Malcolm*, 34.
16. Ibid., 73.
17. Ibid., 74.
18. Lewis, *English Literature*, 463.

Acknowledgements

Editors incur many debts. Mine are chiefly to Brendon Nielson and Fiona Sherwin, without whom this volume would not have appeared.

1

Convergence in Joy

A Comparison of the Devotional Practices of C. S. Lewis and That "Dreadful Man Karl Barth"

DAVID W. WILLIAMS

THE GAPING CHASM BETWEEN the theologies of C. S. Lewis and Karl Barth once prompted Lewis himself to refer to the Swiss theologian as "a dreadful man called Karl Barth."[1] It had shocked Lewis to discover that there were more stern defenders of Christian doctrine against what he called "slush" than himself. The Barthians were so severe it made even Lewis's famed sternness seem like slush. Their preoccupation with judgment, their dismissal of reason, and their assertion that human righteousness was like

---

1. This was written in a letter to Lewis's brother on February 18, 1940: "Did you fondly believe—I did—that where you got among Christians, there, at least, you would escape (as behind a wall from a keen wind) from the horrible ferocity and grimness of modern thought? Not a bit of it. I blundered into it all, imagining that I was the upholder of the old, stern doctrines against modern quasi-Christian slush: only to find that my 'sternness' was their 'slush.' They've all been reading a dreadful man called Karl Barth, who seems the right opposite number to Karl Marx. 'Under judgment' is their great expression. They all talk like Covenanters or Old Testament prophets. They don't think human reason or human conscience of any value at all: they maintain, as stoutly as Calvin, that there's no reason why God's dealings should appear just (let alone merciful) to us: and they maintain the doctrine that all our righteousness is filthy rags with a fierceness and sincerity which is like a blow in the face." Lewis, *Collected Letters II*, 350–51.

filthy rags was handled with a ferocity and a sincerity which was like a smack in the face. And he laid the blame squarely at Barth's feet.

Lewis may have been surprised then that in their actual practice of spiritual devotion, he and Barth shared many points of convergence. These occurred most clearly in the key area of joy, and their shared belief that God was its source and its goal, a discovery Lewis had made later in life but which remained a fundamental aspect of his work. A closer examination of their devotional practices also highlights that for both Lewis and Barth there is no separation between theology and life. Theology happens where life happens. Conversation with God takes place anywhere and everywhere, and all of life becomes parabolic of God's involvement with his creation.

This essay compares the "devotional life" of both Lewis and Barth to see how their theologies played out in actual practice. In Lewis we find someone whose quest for joy dominated his life, but for whom, at least in his early years, the search for joy and the practice of religion were two parallel paths. And yet Lewis became known as one of the most prominent Christian writers, whose large body of work was marked by this overarching theme: the source of joy in all things is the God revealed in Jesus Christ. Ultimately for Lewis, the longing for joy was no less than the longing for glory—to be on intimate terms with God, accepted by God, to find response and acknowledgement, and to be welcomed into the heart of things. Says Wilson: "There is . . . the sense, which informs nearly all his religious writing, that a human being's relationship with God is the great romance of life."[2]

The idea of a devotional life, understood pietistically, was anathema to Barth. Nurtured by liberal theology's conviction that spirituality was inward and subjective, Barth came to believe in a "wholly other" God who could be "had" in no way by human beings. He detested all forms of piety, whether practised by artists or Christians, who to him seemed preoccupied only with the "problems of their private existence."[3] Is it then futile to speak of Barth's devotional life? It is if by "devotional life" is meant the practices people engage in in order to have relationship with God. For Barth that was quite impossible. But if Barth's life and theology is allowed to redefine what is meant by "devotional," then what is discovered is a "wholly other" kind of devotional life and practice. Indeed, if by "devotional life" is meant the space people create in order to discover God's gracious Word afresh, it

---

2. *C. S. Lewis*, 135.
3. Busch, *Karl Barth*, 125.

could be said Barth's entire life was devotional. From his academic career to his pastoral duties, from his love of music and detective novels to his own written work, Barth saw all human life as intersected and struck through by the eternal. For Barth, all of human life was, while perhaps not "sacramental," certainly parabolic. He believed that in the incarnation of His Son, God spoke a definitive word of vindication to His creation—so there was nothing in creation which was not His, and nothing which did not point back to His glory. For this reason, Barth was "suffused with an inner joy,"[4] a joy that he located in the person of God. Just as Lewis would come to realise, the glory of God was not only "great and sublime or holy and gracious . . . it is a glory that awakens joy and is itself joyful."[5]

JOY OR GOD—TWO PATHS MEET

Lewis was exposed early to the practice of Protestant Christianity, but it was rarely favourable. As a boy Lewis had become aware of "experiences," both aesthetic and religious, but neither happened because of Christianity. Church was dull and lifeless—joy was discovered in other places. As Sayer says: "It is not surprising that Jack (Lewis) acquired a dislike of church services and a low opinion of what he knew as Christianity. Of course, he saw no connection between these dull, loveless rituals and his personal religious experience of joy."[6]

Contrasted with the dullness of church life were moments of exhilaration that were happening quite naturally and without effort, and, more importantly, had nothing to do with God or the devotional practices He seemed to demand. Lewis seems to have been uniquely sensitive to an intensity of feeling and his own responsiveness to nature. Sayer compares Lewis to the poet Keats, who needed to nurture his sensibility to experience. Lewis had no such need. "It came to him unbidden when he was young and was at times so strong that he was frightened of madness. But usually it was a source of delight."[7]

One of the first of such unbidden experiences was at the sight of a garden his brother Warren had made from a biscuit tin and covered with moss, twigs and flowers. Says Lewis, "that was the first beauty I ever knew" and

4. Bowden, *Karl Barth*, 22.
5. Ibid., 22.
6. Sayer, *Jack*, 218.
7. Ibid., 78.

"as long as I live my imagination of Paradise will retain something of my brother's toy garden."[8] Lewis came to describe the feeling that accompanied such experiences as "joy," and as he grew his experiences of joy took more shape, becoming associated more particularly with science fiction and carnal lust. Science fiction was, for Lewis, "an intense passion that made him feel almost drunk, a passion he describes as a coarse, heady attraction to be exorcised, more a lust than a genuinely imaginative experience."[9] He was also discovering that females and sexual fantasy produced the same heady passion: "On one occasion he tells us that he felt an electric thrill of lust for a teacher of dancing. . . . This susceptibility and sensitivity to beauty lasted much of his life."[10]

Lewis had discovered early the exhilaration of beauty and became intent on reawakening the experiences. Though he termed it "joy" he admitted that every experience was fleeting and "left the common world momentarily a desert."[11] What he terms "erotic and magical perversions of joy" were his attempts to fashion beauty to his own desires, actually killing the joy in the process. His search for joy became for him a corruption of joy which constantly bordered on madness. Assessing Lewis's definition of "joy" Beversluis says that "not only is the experience of joy fleeting, but even while it lasts it is a desire for what is absent and never fully possessed."[12] Because the desire is for what is never possessed, the desire itself is what produces more desire, resulting in a spiral of intensity and hunger which never finds an ultimate object.

Lewis became so hungry for more experiences of increasing exhilaration that he pursued with almost rabid intensity a form of passion in all his practices, from masturbation to the saying of prayers: "I set myself a standard. No clause of my prayer was to be allowed to pass muster unless it was accompanied by what I called a 'realisation,' by which I meant a certain vividness of the imagination and the affections. . . . Night after night, dizzy with desire for sleep and often in a kind of despair, I endeavoured to pump up my 'realizations.'"[13] Lewis was thirteen years old, the age he says he "ceased to be a Christian." But the simple fact was that his longing for

---

8. Lewis, *Surprised by Joy*, 14.
9. Sayer, *Jack*, 64.
10. Ibid., 68.
11. Lewis, *Surprised by Joy*, 170.
12. Beversluis, *C. S. Lewis*, 13.
13. Lewis, *Surprised by Joy*, 63–64.

experiences was producing habits which were, at the same time, intensifying his sense of guilt. He had discovered masturbation at Cherbourg school, a discovery described by Sayer as "a violent and wholly successful assault of sexual temptation."[14] Masturbation became the bane of Lewis's life, which is obvious from the prominence he has given it in his own autobiographical work (*Surprised by Joy*) and the prominence given it by biographers such as Sayer and Wilson. Masturbation drove yet another wedge between Lewis's longing for joy and his idea of God. Desperate to be free from the misery of his guilt Lewis turned to prayer. But as Sayer says, the "agony of the struggle intensified the sense of guilt."[15] Praying failed to work—Lewis still lusted, he still masturbated, and he still felt guilty. "He therefore despaired of divine aid and regarded himself as an atheist."[16]

So two distinct paths had formed in Lewis's thinking and practices, what Sayer describes as a "lack of integration" which lasted many years.[17] One was the longing for "joy," which ultimately degenerated into the pursuit of carnal thrills. The other was his dutiful practice of religion, which neither produced joy nor helped him cope with the guilt he felt when he tried to produce it himself. How did he picture God at this time? As a "bogey" who was waiting to torture him for his sins. And as Sayer says, Lewis was "quite prepared to live without belief in a 'bogey who is going to torture me forever,' if he should fail in living up to 'an almost impossible ideal.' The Christian God is 'a spirit more cruel and barbarous than any man.'"[18] This picture of God developed through Lewis's teen years. It continued throughout his Oxford University days, from where he wrote to a friend that "the trouble with God is that he is like a person who never acknowledges your letters and so in time you come to the conclusion either that he does not exist or that you have got his address wrong."[19] Nevertheless, Lewis continued the pretence of Christian belief and practice, soothing his father "by reporting that he was regularly reading lessons in chapel and saying grace before meals in the dining hall. It is unlikely that his father realised that this was one of the routine of duties of a scholar of the college."[20]

14. Sayer, *Jack*, 68.
15. Ibid.
16. Ibid., 84.
17. Ibid., 218.
18. Ibid., 113.
19. Ibid., 158.
20. Ibid., 150.

Lewis's intense longing for joy flourished during periods of intense unhappiness at school away from his family. Physical and emotional abuse seem to have marked his early school days, combined with a rigid form of Christian devotional practice. When his mother died Lewis had begged God to save her, convinced that the intensity of his prayers would produce a form of magical cure. Her death was not enough to crush his faith at that stage, because "the belief into which I had hypnotised myself was too irreligious for its failure to cause my religious revolution."[21] Nevertheless, as well as seeing God as a being without joy, Lewis also saw God as a being which does not respond to human grief. In other words, God is a being divorced from all human affections. Why love a being who cannot feel love? As Lewis admits, he "had approached God, or my idea of God, without love, without awe, even without fear."[22]

And yet, the two discrete paths, the search for joy and the practice of religious devotion, started to converge. It happened not with a sermon or a reading of the Bible or prayer, but with the chance purchase of a novel by Scottish universalist preacher and author George MacDonald. While Lewis would not have described it so at the time, MacDonald's *Phantastes* combined joy and religion (or faith) in Lewis's imagination for the first time. But, more extraordinarily, it also awakened in Lewis the sense that joy was inseparable from the story itself. Later, Lewis would describe the event as a baptism of his imagination, the realisation that joy and imagination go hand in hand. What is interesting is that the moment of this realisation as a writer was the moment Lewis as a "Christian" was awakened to holiness—that the world had been redeemed by a God whose own joy could be known in all things: "I now perceived that while the air of the new region made all my erotic and magical perversions of Joy look like sordid trumpery, it had no such disenchanting power over the bread upon the table or the coals in the grate. That was the marvel."[23] For the first time since early childhood an experience of joy did not leave Lewis dissatisfied with life—it heightened his appreciation of it.

However, it was some years before Lewis would describe the experience as "holiness." As Sayer says, "He responded to MacDonald's holiness without recognising it as holiness and at the same time indulged in

21. Lewis, *Surprised By Joy*, 26.
22. Ibid., 26.
23. Ibid., 170.

sadomasochistic fantasies and blasphemous rationalisations."[24] Lewis turned not to God but to the "supreme spirit," convinced of the spiritual realities behind his experiences of joy but refusing to acknowledge they might have anything to do with the Christian God. He even stated that "the experience of the absolute 'is more religious than many experiences that have been called Christian.'"[25] But it was an essential step in Lewis's discovery of God—it was a step outside of himself, beyond the self he had been convinced was the source of joy. At the time, around 1926, his myth *Dymer* was published, which was described by one critic as Lewis's search for his "poetic muse," or the voice outside him which was the source of his imaginings: "Only the death of Lewis-the-romantic-dreamer can make possible the birth of his new literary vision, one based, not on self-centred fantasy, but ultimately on God, the great and true romantic."[26] They were prophetic words.

It was another five years before Lewis became a believer in Jesus Christ as the incarnate son of God. He had always struggled with the idea of a God who had taken flesh, but as his two paths finally converged upon the fact that Jesus, a man, was God it ceased to be merely a difficult doctrine, and became a wide open doorway to a whole new way of seeing life, joy, glory and holiness: "He was derisively called a romantic. . . . It was true in the sense that Lewis had open eyes and had not, like most of us, lost his capacity for wonder at the way of things. The fact that God was made flesh disclosed to Lewis a sanctity in the commonplace and everyday."[27]

Understanding Lewis's sense of holiness in the commonplace and everyday is the key to understanding and learning from his devotional practices after this time. Once the paths had converged and he saw all life as sanctified he could view prayer, reading of the Bible and the taking of sacraments as participation in the life of God even when it did not feel particularly "spiritual." He viewed all of life as sacramental, pointing to the glory of God behind all things. He recognised holiness in the most normal of practices, learning to pray and praise in any and every circumstance, while also remaining deeply committed to standing against any sort of empty ritual for its own sake. Sayer sums up the change: "Jack's conversion to Christianity made him a different person. His search for belief was over;

24. Sayer, *Jack,* 218.
25. Ibid., 220.
26. Ibid., 213.
27 Kilby, *Christian World,* 12.

he now had a strong platform on which to stand. No longer an introspective young man, he became far more confident in his work as a tutor. He devoted himself to developing and strengthening his belief, and almost from the year of his conversion, he wanted to become an evangelist for the Christian faith."[28]

Of his lifetime search for joy, Lewis said he lost all interest in the subject once he became a Christian: "I now know that the experience, considered a state of my own mind, had never had the kind of importance I once gave it. It was valuable only as a pointer to something other and outer. While that other was in doubt, the pointer naturally loomed larger in my thoughts."[29]

BEGIN WHERE YOU ARE—LEWIS'S DEVOTIONAL LIFE

After his conversion Lewis began a devotional life which reflected the convergence of the two paths. He was convinced that if God had become flesh then he, Lewis, need not adopt any airs and graces to approach Him. He could speak as he was, with all his faults, sins, troubles, grievances. Gone was his attempt at "realisation" and drumming up affections. He was committed to being himself before God. For example, he could admit that his own moodiness would affect how he prayed and worshipped; he was convinced a person should lay before God what was in them, not what ought to be in them; he did not like what he called "ready-made" prayers; he believed that a person should begin to pray wherever they were at the time, not to try and prepare some hallowed ground.

Lewis's *Letters to Malcolm* outline many of his broad ideas about the devotional life. On why a person should pray Lewis said that in prayer "instead of being merely known, we show, we tell, we offer ourselves to view."[30] He also spoke of prayer the way he spoke of reading stories; that prayer enriches our appreciation of life. This is no surprise, since Lewis came to realise there was no faith without imagination, something he learnt from Tolkien: "One great value of prayer is that it forces us to leave the continually impinging secularism of life and awaken to the 'smell of Deity' which hangs over it. In prayer, as in the Lord's Supper, we take and eat. Understanding,

28. Sayer, *Jack*, 231.
29. Lewis, *Surprised by Joy*, 224.
30. Lewis, *Letters to Malcolm*, 33.

desirable as it may be, is for the time replaced by a contact with ultimacy."[31] This contact with ultimacy, with the glory behind the beauty, remained a priority for Lewis. Convinced of the promise of glory behind the most secular of activities he was committed in prayer and devotion to tasting heaven: "[In our desire for the spiritual] we are only claiming to know that our apparent devotion . . . was not simply erotic, or that our apparent desire for heaven . . . was not simply a desire for longevity or jewellery or social splendours."[32] The convergence of the paths had, for Lewis, given things a new value. His devotional practices were not acts of blind obedience, but a space in which he might experience holiness itself: "Perhaps we have never really attained at all to what St Paul would describe as spiritual life. But at the very least we know . . . that we are trying to use natural acts and images and language with a new value, have at least desired a repentance which was not merely prudential and a love which was not self-centred,"[33] Sayer sums up Lewis well when he says "When he became a Christian he found that his life had a new centre and what he hoped would be a new stability."[34]

So much for the why. What of the how? Lewis seems to have written little about the mechanics of his prayer and devotional life, but friends remembered his idiosyncrasies. Sayer remembered him spending time in prayer and the Bible early in the day:

> When we got home, he would go to his bedroom and wash thoroughly. He rarely had a bath when he was staying with me, and I think less often still at the Kilns. If there was not already one in his room, he would then ask for a Bible "in any translation" and say his prayers. he found this the best time of the day for them. . . . I think he was always awake when I took him a cup of tea at half past seven, and I think he was usually praying.[35]

Lewis said that wherever possible he would avoid praying in the evening, since sleepiness would overcome him. He had no trouble praying while traveling or in public, but preferred to pray kneeling, since "the body ought to pray as well as the soul. Body and soul are both the better for it."[36]

---

31. Kilby, *Christian World*, 165.
32. Quoted in Griffin, *C. S. Lewis*, 225.
33. Lewis, "Transposition," 78.
34. Sayer, *Jack*, 227.
35. Ibid., 342, 344.
36. Lewis, *Prayer*, 29.

A MYTH RETOLD

Ever aware of body and soul being inseparable, Lewis's devotional life was experiential, even mystical, and yet grounded in the practical:

> My own plan, when hard pressed, is to seize any time and place, however unsuitable, in preference to the last waking moment.... On a day of travelling... I'd rather pray sitting in a crowded train than put it off till midnight when one reaches a hotel bedroom with aching head and dry throat.... On other and slightly less crowded days a bench in a park, or a back street where one can pace up and down, will do.[37]

On how he structured his prayers, Lewis said that imagination was essential. According to Wilson, Tolkien "had taught him that the inability to believe in Christianity was primarily a failure of the imagination. This insight had enabled Lewis to recover all the things in art and in life which he had been enjoying since imaginative awareness dawned."[38] So, Lewis would speak of the mental images which played an important part in his praying: "I doubt if any act of will or thought or emotion occurs in me without them. But they seem to help me most when they are most fugitive and fragmentary—rising and bursting like bubbles in champagne or wheeling like rooks in a windy sky."[39]

According to Kilby, Lewis believed that "prayer must include confession and penitence, adoration and fellowship with God as well as petition,"[40] but he did leave time for petition, since "he had a lengthy list of people for some of whom he had prayed over a long span of years and some of whom he knew simply as 'that old man at Crewe' or 'the waitress' or even 'that man.'"[41]

Lewis's pattern of prayer changed when he married Joy Davidman in 1956. During her sickness in 1957 Lewis would pray for "long periods of time, not only for her but also for the ability to be a substitute, to take some of her pain on himself."[42] Joy died in July 1960, and Lewis felt both "paralysed and obsessed. He was unable to pray in his own words. He was reduced to repeating conventional or 'infantile' prayers. He was quite unable

---

37. Ibid., 28.
38. Wilson, *C. S. Lewis*, 135.
39. Lewis, *Prayer*, 113.
40. Kilby, *Christian World*, 159.
41. Ibid.,166.
42. Sayer, *Jack*, 369.

to write."[43] Again, it seems Lewis's prayer life was inextricably bound to his creative imagination, and both were bound to the events of life. The price he paid for seeing the sanctity of the incarnation in all things, especially his wife, was the extraordinary pain of its loss when it had gone. After her death Lewis spoke of Joy in mystical terms, of knowing and loving "the Her." "Somehow it reopens to him his relationship with God and deepens his faith. He can think of her good qualities and turn from her to Him who made her."[44] Lewis was able to see his wife sacramentally even in the memory of her. Writes Gresham, their love "grew from the more conventional love of a man for a woman and a woman for a man, until it became something indescribable in human terms, a great and holy glorification of God's gift to mankind."[45] In *A Grief Observed* Lewis wrote that Joy's absence was like the sky, "spread over everything."[46] The book also outlines Lewis's brief but outspoken anger against God for not providing Joy with a second miracle cure. "He confessed that his bitter words against God the night before were 'a yell rather than a thought.'"[47]

A Grief Observed was not the only work influenced directly by his dynamic relationship with God. Throughout his career, from before and after his conversion, his search for joy and his ultimate discovery that God was the source, would shape all his work, most noticeably in his religious writings, but also in his fiction.

IMAGINATION REDEEMED—LEWIS'S LITERARY VISION

Lewis was a prolific writer of Christian material following his conversion, but his personal view was that less books were needed about Christianity, and more books by Christians on other subjects "in which the Christianity was latent."[48] This was consistent with his theology of the incarnation, whereby even the most secular images could speak of the holiness and glory of God (to those with the eyes of faith to see). According to Sayer, Lewis "wanted the moral and spiritual significance of his works of fiction to be

---

43. Ibid., 393.
44. Ibid.
45. Gresham, *Lenten Lands,* 112.
46. Quoted in Kilby, *Christian World,* 122.
47. Ibid., 23.
48. Sayer, *Jack,* 256.

'assimilated' subliminally, if at all."[49] For his efforts though, Lewis came to be seen as a Christian writer, and even his most famous fictional work, the Narnia series, would be read less for its fantasy, and more for its allegory. Though the work has broad appeal, and the non-Christian would rarely guess the deeper significance of the characters and events, it is too typically reduced to what it represents, in a way Lewis was against.

Not that the gospel is not weaved through the Narnia Chronicles. The series remains the best example from his work of how his view of God and the work of redemption touched his imagination, while retaining the integrity of the story and characters. As Kilby says, in *The Lion, the Witch and the Wardrobe*, particularly, "there is seldom the sense of contrived situations for didactic purposes."[50] While elements of the books have been severely criticised, even by his friend Tolkien, the Narnia Chronicles highlight more than anything Lewis's view of Christ, in the character of Aslan the lion. Lewis said of Aslan that the reason his passion moves readers more than the real story in the Gospels is that "it takes them off their guard."[51] As Kilby notes, "to take people off their guard was, of course, Lewis's hope, not only in the children's stories but in all his Christian writings."[52]

What takes people off their guard with the character of Aslan is his unpredictability and dynamic interaction with the children. His character is not easily explained, and if you consider that he is the "Christ-figure" in the story, then elements of his character become troublesome—and yet consistent with the multi-faceted representation of Christ in the gospels. At times Aslan is gentle and safe, but at others the children are reminded he is, after all, untamed. At other times he catches them out with humour. Lewis had grown up with a view of God that was predictable and sterile, too bound to a dry reading of the *Book of Common Prayer* and devoid of human emotion. The discovery that God was in fact the author of all human emotion and through the incarnation was bound up with the human dilemma and the inconsolability of its longing for glory, "baptised" his imagination and caused him to rethink all that he knew of God. So, "there are no easy and slick explanations of Aslan's conduct."[53] Sayer quotes Lewis's friend Bede Griffiths summing up the character of Aslan: "The figure of Aslan

49. Ibid.
50. Kilby, *Christian World*, 136.
51. Quoted in ibid., 136.
52. Ibid.
53. Ibid.

tells us more of how Lewis understood the nature of God than anything else he wrote. It has all the hidden power and majesty and awesomeness which Lewis associated with God, but also all the glory and the tenderness and even the humour which he believed belonged to Him."[54]

THE GOD OF ALL PERFECTIONS

There was not a time when Karl Barth was not confronted with the question of God. His earliest theological instruction came at the age of three, from the children's songs of a theologian called Abel Burckhardt who had lived a hundred years before. Barth said of the songs, they "were the textbook from which I received my first theological instruction . . . in a form which was appropriate for my immature years."[55] Barth may have been only three, but the songs made a lasting impression. Sung to him by his mother, they struck Barth by their earthiness, the self-assurance with which they recounted the events of the gospel story, from Christmas to Pentecost. "History? Doctrine? Dogma? Myth? No. It was all things actually taking place. You could see everything for yourself, listen to it and take it to heart by hearing one of these songs sung in the language you were hearing elsewhere and beginning to speak, and you could join in the song itself."[56] Barth the theologian would come to have the same effect on his students and readers. The God he discovered in those songs was a God he would come to speak of with the same earthiness, the same assurance, and the same transcending of "whole oceans of historicism and anti-historicism, mysticism and rationalism, orthodoxy, liberalism and existentialism."[57] He would come to be a truly "evangelical" theologian.

Side-by-side with the gospel of the songs was the message of the church, a threat of eternal damnation that seemed at odds with the stories he had come to know through the songs. Barth says, "I had a well-meaning but rather silly Sunday School mistress who thought it proper to give us children a precise description of hell and the eternal torments waiting there for the wicked. Of course, this interested us and excited us quite a lot but none of us there at the time learnt the fear of the Lord and the beginning

---

54. Quoted in Sayer, *Jack,* 319.
55. Busch, *Karl Barth* , 8.
56. Ibid.
57. Ibid., 9.

of wisdom in this way."[58] Barth's future theological course was set in these early years and shaped by these experiences. He discovered as a child the emptiness of the threat of hell, and the beauty of the gospel story. It is no coincidence that he would come to see God not as the fearful tyrant who demands obedience, but as the "God of all perfections," who awakens joy and love.[59] It is something in God himself "which justifies us in having joy, desire and pleasure towards Him, which indeed obliges, summons and attracts us to do this."[60]

Before he came to this conclusion however, Barth would follow a path of theological instruction which threatened to strip the gospel he knew of its earthiness and joy. Against his father's wishes he committed himself to the study of liberal theology, falling under the instruction of German theologian Adolf von Harnack, for whom Christianity was no more than one of many movements in man's history of religious thought, and Wilhelm Herrmann, a pupil of Schleiermacher's subjective spirituality. Barth had determined to be a theologian from the eve of his confirmation in 1902. He had developed some "rather holy ideas"[61] and wanted to pursue theology in order to get a proper understanding "from within" of the creeds he had been confessing.[62] Barth's fixation was on getting behind the nature of things, particularly the church's doctrines.

Barth was both "curious and thirsting for knowledge,"[63] and in 1910 became a pastor whose sermons were both "very academic" and "very liberal."[64] Interestingly, his messages, however "liberal" Barth may have considered them, would not be out of place in many modern evangelical contexts. For Barth, "liberal" meant subjective. The thrust of his message was this: "The greatest thing is what takes place in our hearts."[65] Christianity was a religious conviction, and its main concern was with moral behaviour and personal spirituality. His purpose as a pastor was to "ask God to make Christ ever richer and clearer in our midst. Then all of us

---

58. Ibid., 14.
59. Bowden, *Karl Barth*, 23.
60. Quoted in ibid.
61. Busch, *Karl Barth*, 31.
62. Ibid.
63. Ibid., 46.
64. Ibid., 54.
65. Ibid.

together, congregation and pastors, will be able to be something like friends and brothers and sisters to each other."[66]

Events associated with the Great War awakened Barth to the realisation that stirrings of the human heart and manifestations of the spirit of Christ among congregations were not the point of Christianity at all. His ideas of God came undone when his theological masters, Harnack, Herrmann, and others, identified themselves among ninety-three German intellectuals who supported the German war policy. Barth regarded the manifesto as the weakness of his teachers in the face of the ideology of war. "Their 'ethical failure' indicated that 'their exegetical and dogmatic presuppositions could not be in order.' Thus 'a whole world of exegesis, ethics, dogmatics and preaching . . . was shaken to the foundations.'"[67] In the months which followed Barth hit another crisis—how to use the Bible to speak of the kingdom of God now that his liberal presuppositions had come crashing down. He should return to academic theology, he told his lifelong friend Eduard Thurneysen, since his own intellectual resources needed to be expanded. "What we need for preaching, instruction and pastoral care," responded Thurneysen, "is a 'wholly other' theological foundation."[68]

Barth's "wholly other" foundation would come from Romans: "I sat myself under an apple tree and began to apply myself to Romans with all the resources that were available to me at the time. . . . I began to read it as though I had never read it before. I wrote down carefully what I discovered, point by point. . . . I read and read and wrote and wrote."[69] What Barth discovered in Romans was God. Not the appropriate Christian thoughts about God, but God Himself, and not in a mystical or "spiritual" way, but dialectically—caught in the interplay between these two opposing truths: humans cannot know God, and God has made Himself known. Barth says he discovered a God who is really God:

> Not a fifth wheel on the wagon but the wheel that drives all the rest. . . . Not a notion, not a view, but the power of life which overcomes the powers of death. . . . Not an adornment to the world, but a lever which is applied to the world! Not a feeling with which one toys, but a fact which one takes seriously. . . . Only now do we

---

66. Ibid., 52.
67. Quoted in ibid., 81.
68. Ibid., 97.
69. Ibid.

begin to perceive him, the living God. There can be no question of our knowing him, of our "having" him.[70]

By his own definition, Barth had come to faith, if faith is "the collapse of every effort of [a person's] own capacity and will and the recognition of the absolute necessity of that collapse."[71] No longer could Barth regard any form of subjectivity as the truth, no matter how convincing the feeling. Hence, there was no place in Barth's new theology for a relationship with the "wholly other" God based on any human practice, let alone the devotional or "religious" practices of the pious Christian. Barth was once asked for a description of his spiritual condition, to which he replied: "A man who looks directly into the sun, into the burning radiance, will so injure his eyes that he will see it no more. It is like this also with faith; whoever looks too directly into the holy Christian faith will be astonished and deeply disturbed with his thoughts."[72]

Busch says, "It was the discovery of the Bible which held [Barth's] attention,"[73] and not because the Bible provided him with grounds for a subjective claim on God. He was fascinated not by what the Bible directed him to do at all, but what lay behind the text, or "beneath the crust" as he described it:

> It is not the right human thoughts about God which form the content of the Bible, but the right divine thoughts about men. The Bible tells us not how we should talk with God but what He says to us; not how we find the way to Him, but how He has sought and found the way to us; not the right relation in which we must place ourselves to Him, but the covenant which He has made with all who are Abraham's spiritual children and which He has sealed once for all in Jesus Christ.[74]

So, without reason or desire to have what would conventionally be described as a "devotional life," one could expect Barth's view of God to be dry and impersonal. Not so, says Bowden: "Barth is in love with his subject and how much it brings him a delight that suffuses him with an inner joy."[75] Barth's idea of God was not dry at all, and Barth certainly did not perceive

70. Barth quoted in ibid., 102.
71. Ibid., 172.
72. Barth, quoted in Bowden, *Karl Barth*, 14.
73. Busch, *Karl Barth*, 98.
74. Barth, *Church Dogmatics* II.I, 43.
75. Bowden, *Karl Barth*, 22.

Him as being distant. In fact, what shocked Barth the most was that the human-divine relationship was based solely on God coming very close "in his movement towards humanity in Jesus Christ."[76] And while God was "wholly other" He was certainly not without His own humanity, joy, or even humour. For Barth, these "human" qualities were God's glory: "If a different view of His glory is taken and taught, then even with the best will in the world, and even with the greatest seriousness and zeal, the proclamation of His glory will always have in a slight or dangerous degree something joyless, without sparkle or humour, not to say tedious and there finally neither persuasive nor convincing."[77]

Barth was convinced that God was a God of sparkle and joy. And he became convinced of this not by segmenting his day into periods of secular or sacred activity, some for God, some for himself, but by devoting the entirety of himself and his work to the discovery of the God he met in the pages of scripture; to the prayerful response invited by this God; and to the enjoyment of His joy in all areas of life, whether "religious" or "profane."

THE SIGH OF THE SOUL—BARTH'S DEVOTIONAL LIFE

Considering the vast amount of "serious" theology Barth came to write during his lifetime, it is remarkable that he is remembered not as a serious man at all, but as someone who was playful and carefree. "His whole attitude to life, and even to theology, was expressed in his passionate love for the carefree, light-hearted music of Mozart, in which the profoundest questions are put to the eternal and the creaturely alike without the dogmatic presumption to any final answer or last word."[78] Sharp-tongued to the point of being cruel on occasions, Barth was nevertheless a man of great humour and wit and could easily laugh at himself. After serving as a pastor for ten years, Barth took the seat of professor of theology at Gottingen University. In his early years as a lecturer, when his theology was taking a beating from both liberals and conservatives, Barth once remarked that "on the black notice board where announcements of lectures were pinned they put mine next to the lessons of the teacher who showed students how to play the harmonium."[79]

76. Hart, *Regarding Karl Barth*, 72.
77. Barth, *Church Dogmatics* II.I, 655.
78. Torrance, *Karl Barth*, 12.
79. Barth quoted in Busch, *Karl Barth*, 133.

Barth was a man with simple tastes, who apart from the odd pipe and a glass of beer or wine was fairly ascetic in his practices. His normal daily routine was to rise early and spend about half an hour in reflection. "Then he would listen for a while to the music of his beloved Mozart from the library of gramophone records with which his friends kept him well supplied."[80] He would read the newspaper each morning and then work until early afternoon. "At 3:45pm, four days a week, he would leave home for his lecture at the university; when that was over he would return to work again, often until well after midnight."[81] Mozart and detective novels were his means of relaxation late at night.

Despite his total dedication to his work, often at the expense of his wife and children, whom he once described as "swarming around and living as though under glass,"[82] Barth was renowned for his love of life—in fact, of all things human, for which he had "an overflowing delight . . . whether they were the simplicities of natural life or the great achievements of the human spirit."[83] Every Saturday Barth would go for walks with groups of students during which he either "taught and walked or walked and taught."[84] "At Christmas Barth once delighted them by giving them 'biscuits, cigars and a copy of Romans,' one each for the flesh, the soul and the spirit."[85] He loved nature, particularly the ocean, remarking once that "blue is the colour, in particular the theological colour."[86] But music was his great passion. He first heard music played by his father, a couple of bars from The Magic Flute: "They went right through me and into me, I don't know how, and I thought, 'That's it!'"[87]

As Torrance says, "One of the most striking things about Karl Barth was his sheer *Menschlichkeit* or humanity. . . . He manifested a frankness and childlikeness and sincerity toward other human beings, which could be both gentle and rough, but always with compassion."[88]

---

80. Bowden, *Karl Barth*, 9.
81. Ibid.
82. Barth quoted in Busch, *Karl Barth*, 163.
83. Torrance, *Karl Barth*, 12.
84. Busch, *Karl Barth* , 130.
85. Ibid., 132.
86. Ibid., 187.
87. Ibid., 15.
88. Torrance, *Karl Barth*, 12.

CONVERGENCE IN JOY

In fact, Barth could be said to have been gifted with the same "farseeing happy patience" he once ascribed to Jesus. It is only in such a happy patience that all things transitory, "even in their abnormal forms, are seen in the light of the eternal."[89] Barth saw all of life in relation to eternity, because he was convinced that in the incarnation all of life had been redeemed. The everyday events of life were "in their way fully justified, inevitable and complete."[90] In other words, life was sacramental, or parabolic—it pointed back to God because the incarnation had already taken place; reconciliation between God and creation had already been achieved. So Barth could exhort Christians to overflow with humanity. Far from exhorting others to live under the cloud of judgment, as suggested by Lewis in his comment to this brother, Barth in fact exhorted Christians to be "more romantic than the romanticists and more humanistic than the humanists. . . . Only that man can speak as Jesus speaks . . . who in perfect peace can recognise in the worldly the analogy of the heavenly."[91]

Barth was committed to the Bible because it was only there that humanity could discover the God who had redeemed the world in Christ. A god proclaimed anywhere else, whether in the human heart or in the history of religions, was a god served by human hands. For Barth theology was not merely talk about God, but a human response "to the word of God that has already been spoken to man before theology begins."[92] So Barth "bent all his energies and talents to let the Word of God bear critically upon himself so that he might be able to hear a genuine word of God's grace."[93] He was like the people of the Psalms, who "meditate on the law day and night."[94] Barth knew that any word other than the one heard in the Bible would ultimately be confounded by anyone "with something they wanted to tell themselves."[95] And so he was vehemently opposed to any form of inward reflection as Christian practice. Barth once spoke to a group of women teachers on his thoughts about religious instruction. "His clear criticism of 'religion' here (as a private affair, as mere inwardness, as

---

89. Barth, *The Word Of God*, 305.
90. Ibid., 304.
91. Ibid., 303, 305.
92. Bowden, *Karl Barth*, 13.
93. Torrance, *Karl Barth*, 5.
94. Busch, *Karl Barth*, 130.
95. Torrance, *Karl Barth*, 5.

a quietist, ineffective attitude) is striking. Religion, he argued, by-passes life—life in the world and even more life in the Bible."[96]

For Barth, to be non-religious was to be fully human, embracing all of life, and all of God's grace. To be non-religious also meant praying. Barth himself said that theology could be performed "only in the act of prayer."[97] Peterson says that since it is "the Holy Spirit who does the forming in spiritual formation, the one essential thing that we do is pray, submitting ourselves to the Spirit's formation."[98] Barth was a theologian who prayed, and "the praying is continuously woven in and out of his writing."[99] For Barth, praying was not so much an activity as a stance, a continuous sighing before the God whom we can never possess: "There is more hope when we sigh *veni creator spiritus* than when we exult as though the Spirit were already ours. You have been introduced to my theology when you have heard this sigh."[100]

Barth did make space and time for prayer. He saw prayer as a sabbath rest, a break in the cycle in order to respond to the God who had already addressed him in Jesus. The theologian's work should pause in order for them to turn their attention away from their own efforts for a moment: "A special measure must obviously be taken; the circular movement must be interrupted; a sabbath day must be inserted and celebrated. . . . At such a moment [the theologian] can and should turn exclusively toward the object of theology, himself, to God. . . . Every prayer has its beginning when a man puts himself . . . out of the picture."[101]

So while Barth eschewed the pietists' commitment to a devotional life, he himself set aside time for devotional practices. The difference was, Barth did not see these times as having any more capacity to manifest God than any other area of his life, whether that was lecturing or sailing, praying or smoking a pipe. For Barth, all of life was bound up together in the miracle of the incarnation. And this miracle was the basis on which he could read scripture, pray, listen to Mozart, or write theology.

Bromiley describes Barth's *Church Dogmatics* in words which could also be used to describe Barth's "devotional" life: "This is not the theology

---

96. Busch, *Karl Barth*, 102.
97. Barth, *Evangelical Theology*, 160.
98. Peterson, *Take and Read*, 34.
99. Ibid.
100. Barth quoted in Busch, *Karl Barth*, 139.
101. Barth, *Evangelical Theology*, 162.

of a man and his thoughts about God. It is the theology of a man meeting God and responding to Him."[102] It was Barth's stance before God (i.e., his sigh) that made his written work so characteristic. He is so filled with wonder that when Barth writes about God the reader wants to meet Him and respond to Him in the same way. To read Barth is to be swept up into something so much bigger than yourself. As Bromiley says, "Barth as a rhetorician can achieve magnificent flights. The freshness and vigour of his statements add to his theology the force and vitality of holy scripture and the best reformation writing."[103]

Peterson suggests the freshness and vigour of Barth's writing is because Barth himself was so full of joy. Barth blessed God. He was so grateful, that when he wrote the gratitude oozed from the page. Like a wide-eyed child he wrote out of wonder, overflowing with the joy and humour, the "happy patience," he had discovered in God. "He is one of the great theologians of all time, but the really attractive thing about him is that he was a man who blessed God. His mind was massive, his learning immense, his theological industry simply staggering. . . . Impressive as that is, what is far more impressive, to me at least, is what he called *dankbarkeit*, gratitude."[104]

The lightheartedness attributed to Barth is echoed even in his most serious work. Peterson describes it as the "chuckle rumbling underneath his most serious prose; there is a twinkle on the edges of his eyes—always. He never took himself seriously and always took God seriously, and therefore he was full of cheerfulness, exuberant with blessing."[105] Unlike Billy Graham, who shocked Barth with his tactics of fear and judgement, Barth's words always conveyed the idea that he was responding to God's grace. Grace is not merely the object of theological reflection in Barth's work, it is the tone, purpose, and the perspective undergirding it all. It is Barth's way of seeing. "Because he refused to take himself seriously, Barth burdened neither himself nor those around him with the gloomy, heavy seriousness of ambition or pride or sin or self-righteousness. Instead, the lifting up of hands."[106]

---

102. Bromiley, *Introduction*, 249.
103. Ibid.
104. Peterson, *A Long Obedience*, 196.
105. Ibid.
106. Ibid.

CONCLUSION

Lewis and Barth were not quite so different as Lewis's comment to his brother suggested. Indeed, in their appreciation of the richness of the redeemed life, their experience of joy, and their belief that all of life was parabolic, they resonated strongly with one another.

The other key area in which Lewis and Barth converge is their writing—their joy overflowed into their written work. Before his conversion Lewis's work was scored by a fruitless search for the deeper truth of things. Lewis confesses that one of his earliest works, *Loki Bound*, was shot through with his atheistic contradictions: "I was at this time living, like so many atheists or antitheists, in a whirl of contradictions. I maintained that God did not exist. I was also very angry with God for not existing. I was equally angry with him for creating the world."[107] After his conversion, according to Wilson, it was as if Lewis had been completed as a writer: "There is no doubt that until he discovered this clothing (be it artificial carapace or 'the whole armour of God') Lewis was only half-formed as a writer, as a literary imagination, perhaps as a person."[108] Rather than fighting a God he claimed not to believe in, Lewis had submitted to a God he had discovered. It was this sense of submission, to God as the source of the joy he had sought to discover for himself, that critics recognised as a recurring theme in his post-conversion work. Says Sayer of *Perelandra*, Lewis's favourite science fiction novel, "One theme is that human beings can only be happy if their wills and all other aspects of their nature are in a state of happy submission to the God."[109]

Lewis had discovered this state of happy submission for himself, which he states so confidently in one of his most memorable Christian works, *The Weight of Glory*: "To please God . . . to be a real ingredient in the divine happiness . . . to be loved by God, not merely pitied, but delighted in as an artist delights in his work or a father in a son—it seems impossible, a weight or burden of glory which our thoughts can hardly sustain. But it is so."[110]

Whether in sermon, lecture, or dogmatics, what stands out in Barth is that "there is no hint that [he] is labouring under a heavy burden."[111] It is a

---

107. Lewis, *Surprised by Joy*, 113.
108. Wilson, *C. S. Lewis*, 124.
109. Sayer, *Jack*, 297.
110. Lewis, *The Weight of Glory*, 97.
111. Bowden, *Karl Barth*, 22.

joy for Barth to write about God, and it is this joy which compelled him to write so much, with such humour and warmth, and in such a dynamic way. "Barth was a master at words, at throwing up verbal pictures and images, at pointing phrases."[112] He has been described variously as an architect of language, a poet, or a painter. Torrance (1990) says he is to Christian theology today what Shakespeare is to English literature and what Mozart is to classical music. What is certain is that, as Bowden says, "Whether it is a long stretch of systematic thinking or a short sermon or an autobiographical article for a journal, the piece is conceived as a whole, so that as one reads it is possible to sense and enjoy the magnificent craftsmanship that has been employed."[113]

For all of the craftsmanship that went into Lewis's and Barth's work, it would not have scaled the heights that it did had they not been writing about something worthwhile. That something is the beauty behind all of life because of the God who has made his presence felt in it. The ability they both possess to see this is summed up beautifully in what Bowden says about Barth: they were able to "set down what has escaped less penetrating eyes."[114]

Both Lewis and Barth could see things no one else could. And to read their work is to have your eyes opened.

---

112. Ibid., 20.
113. Ibid., 23.
114. Ibid.

2

Corresponding Theologically with C. S. Lewis

GEOFFREY HOLT

THE NAME OF C. S. Lewis is respected across denominational and theological boundaries and is a focal point of veneration by some. As an example Paul Holmer states, "His theology, if that is what you call it, is of a quality with the New Testament literature itself."[1] Lewis cultivated a denominational and political neutrality all of his life and was very particular about not only what he did say in public but also what he did not say believing that his usefulness was dependent on staying clear of theological fights between different Christian positions.[2] His popularizing of theology is even more remarkable since he did not read newspapers, or magazines, listen to the radio, or watch television.[3] He also did not, or could not, "make much" of modern theology such as Tillich, Brunner, or Niebuhr.[4] In general he felt as though he was a man out of his time, referring to himself as a dinosaur,[5] and was comedically contemptuous of those who demanded currency. "Incidentally, what is the point of keeping in touch with the con-

---

1. Holmer, *C. S. Lewis*, 107.
2. Lewis, *Collected Letters III*, 1424.
3. Ibid., 667, 984, 1108.
4. Ibid., 978.
5. Ibid., 581.

temporary scene? Why should one read authors one does not like because they happen to be alive at the same time as oneself?"[6] His disdain for contemporary theologians was reciprocated, yet despite his popularity and the wealth that it garnered he remained very humble about how much he could help people in his work of theological vulgarization[7] as he termed it, calling himself "Balaam's donkey."[8] He even refused a knighthood, believing it would diminish the effectiveness of his work.[9] In his published work[10] and in his correspondence he describes himself as a layman writing about Christian truths. This Pauline style modesty (1 Corinthians 15:9; Ephesians 3:8) belies the First that he gained from Oxford University in Philosophy and Metaphysics. Few theologians let alone laymen can offer the credentials that Lewis has in the classical understanding of God and humanity. He saw his work as an attempt at putting simply the wisdom of the past eras for a contemporary generation and that his work would fade into obscurity. He held to a very high view of the position of clergy[11] and that they should be the ones to present Christian doctrine to the masses. Lewis viewed himself as a translator of theological concepts[12] and contended that the key to understanding and believing is simplicity.[13] The interesting thing is that his works continue to sell whereas those of other writers, that he thought greater than himself, have faded into the obscurity he foresaw for himself. Despite suffering from the same fear of poverty as his father, Lewis gave away most of the royalties from his popular work to charity. He was especially wary of his own flaws ("beware here of my unsanguine temper, more tempted to sloth than to precipitance, and ready to despond: take my advice always with a grain of salt").[14] All this is to say that he knew who he was and did not mask his life by his work. As such, I contend, there is no discernible hidden agenda with Lewis.

Theology concerns itself with boundaries and definition of meanings. This is not only to say something clearly but also to delimit and to not say

---

6. Ibid., 83.
7. Ibid., 754.
8. Ibid., 1455.
9. Ibid., 147.
10. Lewis, *Fern-Seed and Elephants*, 86.
11. Sayer, *Jack*, 162.
12. Lewis, *Collected Letters II*, 674.
13. Lewis, "Version Vernacular," 515.
14. Lewis, *Collected Letters III*, 369.

something unwanted inadvertently. Lewis's theological non-fiction demonstrates this feature and presents three major defenses of theism that are based on an understanding of human nature. In doing so he has added to the theological corpus argumentation that is still being discussed more than forty years after his death. These three defenses concern arguments based on: morality, reason or supernature, and desire. About the time of the Second World War, Lewis based his theological works, such as *Mere Christianity*, *The Problem of Pain*, and *The Abolition of Man*, primarily around the concept of morality. His work *Miracles* published shortly after the war, and possibly philosophically his most rigorous work, attempts a defense of the Christian faith against Naturalism. Human beings in their ability to reason and observe nature are placing themselves above the natural realm, and therefore have a super-nature. His earliest published work, *The Pilgrim's Regress*, centers on the relational aspect of desire—that is, our longing for relationship, especially in a teleological sense. This concept of desire he would return to in his later non-fictional romances, the Narnia Chronicles, the Space Trilogy and *Till We Have Faces*.

These three aspects of humanity, morality, the reason, and desire, fit closely to the differing Christian conceptions of the "Image of God." The moral view can be described as what a human does, the way they act or what they do, and can be related to the functional view, as least to that of philosophers such as Plato. The rational or substantive view of the Image of God, sees it as being part of our human nature and features highly philosophical integrations, especially Aristotelian with Christianity, often engendering the view that reason is the only pure part of humanity. Relationally, the Image of God is often seen as humanity's ability to operate spiritually with God, as God's ability to communicate with them and they with Him, or as the human ability to communicate with other humans, being based in Genesis 1 and 9 respectively. Given this, one could say that the Image of God was the basis for most of C. S. Lewis's work whether consciously or unconsciously. But this would raise the problem of not coming to terms with author's intention and speaks more about the commentator's brilliance in drawing together a coherent picture and less about the purpose of the author in presenting the material. I have no reason to presume that Lewis based his Christian-oriented work over a lifetime on the Image of God. More likely is that the highest capacities of humanity that most directly relate to the divine are also the things that most engaged Lewis's thought. With Lewis we have a theology "from below" that relates to human experience because it is portrayed in terms of human experience. As Lewis himself says, "People now all seem to want 'a slice of life' (the flaccid, tepid, grey-to-brown shapeless object is a better image than they know) or a 'comment on life.' To me those who merely comment on experience seem far less valuable than those who *add* to it, who make me experience what I never experienced before."[15] There needs to be a way that allows us to see with clarity what he was intending to mean by these vignettes of experience whether fictional or non-fictional.

UTTERLY GALLEY-SLAVE HOUR

As a translator of theology for the masses Lewis's public works were primarily a recitation of things from the past that he thought were important and were neglected in the present. The response to his writing was enormous and generated a vast amount of correspondence to which Lewis responded personally in a methodical manner. There are presently over 3000 extant letters of C. S. Lewis. Many of these letters have been published before in works such as *Letters of C. S. Lewis*, edited by his brother Warren; *Letters to an American Lady*, edited by Clyde Kilby; and the *Latin Letters of Lewis to Don Giovanni Calabria*, edited by Martin Moynihan. However many of the letters of these volumes were excised for the sake of the correspondent's propriety, and in the case of *Letters to an American Lady* even the name of the woman was removed. Walter Hooper, C. S. Lewis's one-time secretary, has compiled all known letters of C. S. Lewis in three volumes, *The Collected Letters of C. S. Lewis*, and unlike previous attempts, nothing was stricken. This compilation now gives us as full and complete record as is currently possible.

Lewis was possibly the most prolific letter writer of the twentieth century. Although the number of letters currently available is vast, it pales by comparison to the actual amount written. His regular practice was to spend an hour or more a day on correspondence, which he termed his "utterly galley-slave hour."[16] On two days of his life when we have only a single letter we know that he had written many more. On one occasion he had written four before his current letter and still had a pile to complete.[17] At another time in 1955 he had written ten letters in the morning and in both

15. Ibid., 918.
16. Ibid., 1076.
17. Ibid., 1431.

occasions they are the only extant letter for the day. We also have no letters from surrounding days. The letters that we do have conservatively, I believe, amount to approximately one in fifty of his total correspondence. That we have so little of his total correspondence lends to problems in providing a complete picture but they still give the hardest evidence of his thought and life that occurred behind his writing. It may be the sad reality that it was the best of his letters that are now lost. This, however, would be to argue from silence. What we do have is an amazing abundance of background material to his works and direct theological interaction with his reader, critics, and friends.

The importance of the documentary nature of correspondence was not lost on Lewis as evidenced by his discussion with his brother concerning the family papers. Lewis wanted the letters arranged chronologically and not with respect to the individual author.[18] He also kept a card index system with the details of his correspondents, including any photos given.[19] He also saw the letters as part of his Christian duty for his fellow human beings, an aid for those in need of assistance.[20] What we have in Lewis's correspondence is the remnant of at least five percent of his life's work, and his pastoral theology from thirty years of ministry experience albeit not ordained. It is surprising, then, that the letters have been largely ignored as obiter dictum when they provide the clearest view of his theology as it developed and was refined by interaction with friends, family, colleagues, and readers.

IF SO I AM A TRANSLATOR

His correspondence is of particular importance in the theological interpretation of his fiction as it is easy to read into any element of a story some theological nuance that the reader believes is there but is simply part of the "yarn." What is clear from his letters is that his fiction starts with an image or images that are later morphed and grouped into a story.[21] For instance, the starting imagery for *The Lion, the Witch and the Wardrobe* was a series of bad nightmares Lewis had concerning a lion.[22] Adults tend to read into

18. Lewis, *Collected Letters II*, 50.
19. Lewis, *Collected Letters III*, 1398.
20. Lewis, *Collected Letters II*, 482; *Collected Letters III*, 109.
21. Lewis, *Collected Letters III*, 503.
22. Ibid., 1245.

a children's story far more than is actually there. As an example, Moorman claims that Lewis has as his reference Augustine's *City of God* in his writing.[23] This is certainly a possibility. Lewis had read this Christian classic and was influenced by Platonic thought as much as Augustine. However, Moorman claims the imagery is simplified so as to preserve the theology upon which it is grounded. Is it not more coherent to say that the imagery is the grounding through which a simplified theology was allowed its scope with all the attached inherent dangers. One of the more recent attempts in like manner to Moorman's thesis is *Planet Narnia: Seven Heavens in the Imagination of C. S. Lewis* by Michael Ward, which seeks an overarching theme for the Narnia chronicles based on cosmology. Ward unlike Moorman had read Lewis's correspondence and chose to totally ignore it believing that he knew the hidden Lewis.[24] The overarching theme that Lewis gave for the Narnia Chronicles after they were all written was Christocentric.[25] Ward dismisses this as false because he can only view Christocentric reading in terms of a historic Christ; that is Ward is looking for salvation history. What Ward was not observing was the unfolding of a pastoral and relational Christ. We know that the Narnia Chronicles did not start with an overarching theme because when Lewis wrote *The Lion, the Witch and the Wardrobe* he did not know he was going to write any more. It was the same with both the sequel *Prince Caspian* and with *The Voyage of the Dawn Treader*; Lewis was sure each would be his last.[26] In each of the stories of the Narnia Chronicles, Lewis moves the characters away from their innate anthropocentric worldview into a Christocentric worldview, and the reader is supposed to follow along with the children. Each of these movements was based around a different theological theme, but the theological theme is more accidental than substantial and only viewed as such in hindsight. Lewis's fictional works are primarily romances designed for people's enjoyment and are only secondarily theological as Lewis himself states, "You must not confuse my romances with my theses. In the latter I state and argue a creed. In the former much is merely supposed for the sake of the story."[27] Much of the scholarship related to Lewis, focuses on his fiction, and attempts to ascertain his theology by way of extrapolating from the characters, plots, settings, and

23. Moorman, *Precincts of Felicity*, 66.
24. Ward, *Planet Narnia*, 11–13.
25. Lewis, *Collected Letters III*, 1244–45.
26. Ibid., 848.
27. Lewis, *Collected Letters II*, 914.

dialogue the theology that the reviewer thinks lies behind these elements. Most often these reviews are mistaken as Lewis himself points out.[28] Lewis also presents things in his fiction that are only tentative so that any element in his novels may be an indication of what he might believe about which he is unsure. This is because in a story one can suggest an idea rather than state it.[29] He also makes this distinction concerning his friend Charles Williams whose mind he termed "undisciplined."[30] Often he describes the process of writing and none of his "stories began with a Christian message. I always start from a mental picture—the floating islands, a faun with an umbrella in a snowy wood, an 'injured' human head."[31] Even with the non-fiction, Lewis had serious doubts about the ability of his reviewers. These doubts are not only presented but are given correction in his letters.[32] The surprising thing was that children were sometimes better than the critics at discerning the theology of Lewis's works.[33] What Lewis was trying to do was present the faith, given in the famous maxim of St. Vincent of Lerins, that it should be for all people, everywhere, at all times; that is a vulgarization of truths that needed contextualizing. While some people thought this work prophetic, Lewis preferred the term, "translator."[34]

This universalistic nature of his writing, especially in his non-fiction, has led many to speculate as to the particulars of the faith that Lewis held. Why is it that Lewis, surrounded by Roman Catholic friends who were instrumental in his conversion, never became a Roman Catholic? Why, since he was so opposed to and scorned by Modernist theologians and endured the difficulties of an alcoholic brother, did he not become a Fundamentalist? Why did he go to Church on a thoroughly regular basis when he could not stand Church life or the hymns that made up much of the service? What are the particular beliefs that opened the door out of the hallway that Lewis chose as his own theological home?[35] To answer these questions we need a scholarship that does not view his letters as irrelevant—that is not looking for a "hidden" Lewis so as to covertly promote their own

28. Lewis, *Collected Letters III*, 289.
29. Ibid., 515.
30. Lewis, *Collected Letters II*, 618.
31. Lewis, *Collected Letters III*, 503.
32. Ibid., 1227.
33. Ibid., 807.
34. Ibid., 1359.
35. Lewis, *Mere Christianity*, xi.

idiosyncrasies or criticize him for what he did not say. Nor is it a matter of delving into his personal life, the *vie-intime* as Lewis put it, that barbarous researchers would ferret out for writing expose biographies.[36] It is interesting to note that there are almost no extant letters between Lewis and Joy Gresham, a correspondence that developed into a close friendship and then finally marriage, and presumably was one of the few correspondents to whom Lewis desired to write. The tendency of many is either to canonize him or to bring charges of heresy, or worse to make aesthetic comments on his style. Lewis was not interested in style unless one was commenting on the substantives of aesthetics. Nor was he interested in being anyone's saint; he knew himself too well, and possibly revered saints too fondly. He was however particularly concerned with heresy, such that he would have his work reviewed by trusted friends. When people claim that Lewis belonged to their own particular theological group, the claim needs careful scrutiny.

IS HE BEGINNING TO SEE PICTURES IN THE FIRE?

Many want to lay claim to Lewis as being covertly their theologian. Two books were written claiming that Lewis was a closet Roman Catholic. Joseph Pearce claims in *C. S. Lewis and the Catholic Church* that Lewis had grown up as a "Belfast bigot," and while Lewis had out grown this he was still not able to shake his upbringing in order to say anything "papist."[37] Christopher Derrick states that Lewis was "sympathetic towards . . . Rome's liturgical paganism, . . . he went to confession, he believed in purgatory and in prayers for the dead; he believed, . . . that Jesus 'vere latiat' in the Eucharist."[38] Lewis's published position was that he thought of himself as "a very ordinary layman of the Church of England, not especially 'high,' nor especially 'low,' nor especially anything else."[39] The problems with the terms "high" and "low" is that they tend to be ill defined and purely relative to the perceived position of the person writing where most think of themselves as being centrist in their views. In many ways his theological position could be described, as J. I. Packer does, as a "conservative Anglican with catholic . . . leanings."[40] This is partly why Roman Catholics do not understand

---

36. Lewis, *Collected Letters III*, 903, 1221.
37. Pearce, *C. S. Lewis*, 100.
38. Derrick, *C. S. Lewis*, 35.
39. Lewis, *Mere Christianity*, v–vi.
40. Packer, "What Lewis Was and Wasn't," 11.

Lewis because they assume that they themselves are representatives of "catholic" theology. Lewis held that the Roman Church had departed from catholic theology; that which is universally held belief, because of its "particular" doctrines. On a more general note Lewis objected, as a logician, to the Roman practice of arguing "from" the truth instead of towards the truth.[41] More pointedly he objected to three particular doctrines, those of the Blessed Virgin Mary, the Papacy, and Transubstantiation.[42] Some suggest that his thinking on these doctrines changed over time, yet between 1945 and 1964 when *Letters to Malcolm* was published there was no change in his view regarding Transubstantiation.[43] Derrick's comments concerning Lewis's use of "vere latiat" is also disingenuous in that it assumes that when Lewis makes a comment concerning the Eucharist, it concerns the host and not the act of taking communion as Cranmerian theology demarcates. When we meet the term as used by Lewis the context is at the end of the sermon "The Weight of Glory," where it is used in regard to one's neighbor who has an eternal soul and in whose company we may meet "Christ."[44] As Transubstantiation is the earliest of Rome's three particularities it seems less likely that the more modern ones of the assumption of Mary and papal infallibility would be countenanced.[45] Lewis's views differed from Roman Catholicism over confession as well. For him it was a beneficial practice to be offered to those who desired it not a universal one to be demanded of all.[46] Although on the surface it may appear that Lewis used practices similar to those of Roman theologians such Pearce and Derrick, the underlying theology and the devotional perception were quite different. This is primarily evident in the aspect of compulsion that underlies much of Roman theology that Lewis finds abhorrent. For Lewis a chief criterion is anthropocentric profitability, does a certain practice help or hinder a person's walk with Christ? This is even true of purgation which Lewis opines as a private matter rather than an essential part of a theological system.[47] I

---

41. Lewis, *Collected Letters II*, 150.
42. Ibid., 646.
43. Lewis, *Letters to Malcolm*, 132.
44. Lewis, "Weight of Glory," 102.
45. Lewis, *Collected Letters II*, 646. "What is most certain is the vast mass of doctrine wh[ich] I find agreed on by Scripture, the Fathers, the Middle Ages, modern R.C.'s, modern Protestants. That is true 'catholic' doctrine. Mere 'modernism' I reject at once."
46. Lewis, *Collected Letters III*, 320.
47. Ibid., 587–88.

would contend that Lewis's stance on this matter is problematic. I do not think he understood the nature of a theological "system" and how purgation is an integral part of the Roman system of salvation and the affront to the theology of penal-substitutionary atonement that underlies the Anglican system of theology to which Lewis had difficulty ascribing.

For Lewis doctrinal differences within the Christian spectrum were of minor import. In his discussion with Griffiths concerning his possible conversion to Rome he states, "One of the most important differences between us is our estimate of the importance of the differences. You in your charity, are anxious to convert me: but I am not in the least anxious to convert you."[48] Conversely he was not a person who wanted to be rid of doctrine and found that those Christians who thought of themselves as "undogmatic and liberal" were the "most arrogant and intolerant."[49] Lewis did not want the differences to stop people having salvation in Jesus Christ, but was offended that people assumed that his refusal to comment on the differences lay in his ignorance.[50] Lewis wanted the Church to be theologically knowledgeable and did not suffer the occurrence of theological creep which he openly disparaged.[51] Theological differences therefore held an importance, but so too was unity. Lewis longed for a reunited Church but could not see how it was to be achieved.[52]

Unlike the claims of Pearce and Derrick, Lewis did not suffer some deep seated angst over his churchmanship. He was neither running from the Ulster Protestantism of his grandfather, nor from the "High Church" of the English public schools that he loathed. His experiences did however make him more open to listen to others who carried different perspectives. For Lewis it was not being an Anglican that mattered. "But the great point is that in one sense there's no such thing as Anglicanism. What we are committed to believing is whatever can be proved from Scripture. On that subject there is endless room for progress."[53] He may not have held to the inerrancy of Scripture, but he was adamant that its authority was greater

---

48. Lewis, *Collected Letters II*, 178.
49. Lewis, *Collected Letters III*, 112.
50. Lewis, *Collected Letters II*, 176.
51. Lewis, *Collected Letters III*, 1592. Theological creep is where the boundaries or definitions of theology are slowly and almost imperceptibly changed over time so that ordinary people do not realize what was intended by the changes that were made and so therefore cannot react against them.
52. Lewis, *Collected Letters II*, 256.
53. Ibid., 647.

than that of Church.[54] He respected and felt close to people of faith not only in Christianity but also had an affinity to Jews and Muslims.[55] One person who can place Lewis within the theological spectrum was not a Christian but a Mormon. Evan Stephenson tells us that Lewis was a prayer book Anglican which is quite correct.[56] Lewis saw good points in the Roman Church thinking it to have more style and finesse and that its record of martyrs for the faith was exemplary but that overall he was unsure as to what God would do with Rome.[57] He was also offended by the tee-totalism of Fundamentalist and Baptist groups even in the midst of dealing with a brother continually hospitalized by alcoholism.[58]

It was not that psychology affected his church going but he wanted the discipline of church attendance even to services he hated to influence his psychology. His personal preference, given in his correspondence, for a style of worship was an Orthodox Church he visited. I would contend, had he decided to alter allegiances, possibly due to the ordination of women, he would possibly have gone to that "door" of the "hallway."[59] Having said this, doctrines such as the invocation of the saints would still have presented a problem for Lewis. In general there was often little that appealed to Lewis regarding a Church service. He disliked the hymns, the people in the pews around him, the giving of notices, and often the Church's clergy themselves.[60] All these things he viewed as opportunities rather than hindrances for spiritual growth. As opposed to Lyle Dorsett who claimed that Lewis "lived in the Church and loved it," Lewis lived in academia and disliked Church.[61] Church life existed in Lewis's conception for a different purpose than Church growth sensibilities dictate. As Lewis exclaimed to Sister Penelope, "I think what really worries me is the feeling . . . that there's really nothing I so much dislike as religion—that it is all against the grain and I wonder if I can really stand it!"[62] Church attendance was for Lewis a rationed duty of prescribed time that took him away from the activities and

---

54. Lewis, *Collected Letters III*, 1307–8.
55. Ibid., 249.
56. Stephenson, "The Last Battle," 51.
57. Lewis, *Collected Letters III*, 477–78, 678.
58. Ibid., 580.
59. Ibid., 720.
60. Ibid., 731, 325, 463.
61. Dorsett, *Seeking the Secret Place*, 78.
62. Lewis, *Collected Letters II*, 497.

important elements of this life.⁶³ Church life was to develop the likeness of Christ in a person from the discipline of doing things that one would not do by nature. It was the place where "[God's] praise is a necessary reaction: the divine light sent back to its Source from the creature which has become its mirror."⁶⁴ His life-long view was that Church in private homes should be avoided, because Church was not primarily about togetherness but the knowledge and worship of God.⁶⁵ Those things that made for distinctive between churches whether considered high or low had each their own value.⁶⁶ Lewis's desire for Church unity was not based on an organic ecumenical union which he thought headed toward disastrous failure but through acts of collective kindness and much prayer.⁶⁷ For Lewis the Church was a place for active love of one's fellow Christians and not a place of passively being in a state of belovedness.

THE PRECIOUS ALABASTER BOX

Lewis focused his theology around personal experience. In this manner he was more Methodist than Anglican, perhaps this was the Welsh heritage he always claimed, more likely it was that he believed one should write about what one knows and that the object of the writer is to make a more expansive world for the reader by allowing the reader to enter an experience they had not yet known. One of the more troubling aspects of Lewis's writing is the belief that worship is based on the goodness of God or else, for Lewis, worship becomes mere terrified flattery. Those parts, therefore, of the Bible which to Lewis's conception present God as somehow less than good must be false.⁶⁸ The problem with this is that it turns worship into the glorification of a deity of one's own design. Lewis himself perceived this problem and realized that our rationalizations of the more mythical elements found in Scripture as he himself viewed them, were always what the rationalization borrowed and that it is to the mythic elements that the mind is drawn because they contain the immediacy of intimacy and experience. Lewis rarely used the word "worship" to describe Church life, preferring

---

63. Lewis, *Collected Letters III*, 1588–89.
64. Lewis, *Collected Letters II*, 970.
65. Lewis, *Collected Letters III*, 1289, 1416.
66. Ibid., 320.
67. Ibid., 1425–26.
68. Ibid., 1436–37.

words such as religion and liturgy, which for him were just a "simulacrum" of the true heavenly worship.[69] Early in his life Lewis viewed himself as "Low Church," because his experience of "High Church" were "v[ery] harsh people who called themselves scholastics and appeared to be inspired more by hatred of their father's religion than anything else."[70] Later he would define "High Church" as a more gracious and less culturally defined way of worshipping.[71] For all his focus on experience he was wary of emotions, that some may delude themselves that the natural emotion associated with music was actually a real religious emotion. "Even genuinely religious emotion itself is only a servant. No soul is saved by having it or damned by lacking it."[72] In the same letter as this quote Lewis gives what I believe are for him the four primary loci of true earthly worship; God-centered, obedient, neighbor-centered, and becoming less self-centered.[73] Obedience was not to the "externalities of religion," nor to "rigid form," nor to self willed religion. Such things Lewis viewed from the vantage point of Colossians 2:23 as being a self-imposed piety or religion. Such externalities are at best just aides for the weak. Obedience is bound to God's grace and differs from religious practice. So, whether one prays seated standing or kneeling is not the issue only that one prays. Religious practices are not the stairwell of sanctification only the banister such that "it is, not the thing by but it is a protective against falling off and a help-up. I think thus we ascend. The stair is God's grace. One's climb from step to step is obedience."[74] Obedience is essential for the establishment and growth of a home, of a business, and of the state, where the only place for disobedience is when what is demanded "of me is contrary to my plain moral duty."[75]

The problem with obedience for Lewis is when it seemed to conflict with being God-centered, such as the difference between Thomas More and William Tyndale, both obedient to their calling unto death, both devout, and as Lewis states, "their disagreement seems to me to spring not from their vices nor from their ignorance but rather from their virtues and the depths of their faith so that the more they were at their best the more they

69. Lewis, *Collected Letters II*, 971.
70. Ibid., 285.
71. Lewis, *Collected Letters III*, 477.
72. Ibid., 731.
73. Ibid., 731–32.
74. Ibid., 342.
75. Lewis, *Collected Letters II*, 371–72; *III*, 21–22.

were at variance."[76] It may be that of course both were wrong, but for Lewis such a discrepancy was the abyssal judgment of God; the phraseology taken from the Vulgate Psalm 35:7. Personally I would have preferred Romans 11:33 in its relation to God but I believe Lewis was focusing on the chasm that separated the two historic figures.

Being God-centered and less self-centered were highlighted for Lewis when he went to Magdalene College in Cambridge. St. Mary's action of breaking an "alabaster box" and pouring it over the feet of Jesus, Lewis took allegorically, that it is our *heart* that must *break* over the feet of Jesus, adding that it was easier said than done and the caveat that "the contents only become perfume only when it is broken. While they are safe inside they are more like sewage. All v[ery] alarming."[77] True theology, that is, knowing God; and the act of worship were both alike alarming, yet it is only these that bring forth peace and fulfillment. The scriptural act is one of singular devotion but taken in allegory it becomes a universal prescription of every act of Christian worship. In Lewis's thought, worship is the most significant act that a human achieves. It is the act towards which theology directs us and from its transforming provenance we live out our lives.

Theology was still for Lewis the queen of the sciences. His letters are filled with the concerns over theology that his works by their nature tend to avoid or subsume. But his correspondence is the locus where we can ascertain particulars of Lewis's theology as he deals with the pastoral concerns of himself, his friends, his readers, and the general public. In a similar way to a person interpreting the theology of St. Paul purely from the book of Acts without reference to his epistles; interpreting C. S. Lewis without his now readily available correspondence seems as pointedly absurd, and prone to possible if not evidential hermeneutical disaster.

---

76. Ibid., 815.
77. Lewis, *Collected Letters III*, 522.

3

Revelation and Natural Theology

ROGER DRIVER-BURGESS

C. S. LEWIS'S WORKS today are much-loved among evangelical Christians. His fiction, for the way in which we are drawn into an adventure story only to find ourselves enjoying the story of Christ, his disciples, and ultimately the redemption of the cosmos; his non-fiction for the vigour and good humour of his arguments and for the experience of hearing opinions that find their roots in the writers of antiquity. In addition, Lewis was an academic and a conservative. He lends an air of respectability to popular conservative opinions, and his more "liberal" views—for example, in regards to the Scriptures—can be passed over in silence.

In more academic contexts we may not pass over uncongenial aspects of our favourite authors in this way. We are, indeed, forced to examine aspects of Lewis that we might rather ignore. For me, there is the troubling thought that Lewis may have adopted a metaphysics, based upon neo-Platonism, that is ultimately at odds with a Reformed theology of revelation. Lewis was consistently engaged with "nature" in his writings; whether in arguing against naturalistic interpretations of particulars, or in finding therein the "good dreams" by which pagan hearts are turned towards God. At a great many points in his writings he is working to explain the relationships between human beings and nature, and human beings as part of nature in relation to the divine.

REVELATION AND NATURAL THEOLOGY

In this essay, I consider the question of whether Lewis at some points adopts a "natural theology," thus rendering the revelation of God by his Word unnecessary, and attacking God's sovereignty by making God a possible object of human knowledge apart from his own action in revelation. The pre-eminent opponent of natural theology remains Karl Barth, with his objection to an analogia entis in modernist and Thomistic theology. I ask to what extent Lewis is guilty of proposing such an *analogia entis*, or, if he is sufficiently free of this particular blot on his escutcheon, what it is that he offers.

I begin this investigation with Lewis's defence of natural law in the short book *The Abolition of Man*, then proceed to consider the essay "Transposition," before turning to his more detailed work, *Miracles*. Along the way I will be asking what these works and others tell us about his methods and his metaphysics, and whether we have due cause for concern as theologians. My ultimate question is whether Lewis's concepts of revelation are sufficiently robust to assuage concerns for God's sovereignty and the uniqueness of his revelation in Christ.

THE ABOLITION OF MAN

In the his 1943 Riddell Memorial Lectures at the University of Durham, later published as *The Abolition of Man,* Lewis enters the lists against what we may describe variously as reductionism, materialism, positivism, or any number of "-isms" by which morality and meaning itself seem to be attacked. These "-isms" may helpfully be called "naturalism" as they were by Lewis, and are characterised by an insistence that phenomena are understood in terms of their own characteristics rather than interpreted according to some external framework of meaning; that is, they are understood according to their own "nature," not according to human ideology. This basic distinction is captured, somewhat simplistically, by Raphael's painting, "The School of Athens," in which the master, Plato, is pointing heavenwards, indicating that phenomena ought to be understood in the light of divine principles, and his student, Aristotle, holds his hand flat over the earth, indicating that they ought to be understood in terms of their own particulars and broader principles generated from the specific instances observed. Lewis, the teacher, takes Plato's view of things. It should be noted at the outset, however, that neither Plato nor Aristotle, nor the Platonic

Augustine or the Aristotelian Thomas, nor Lewis who comes after, can be so simplistically defined.[1]

In chapter 1 Lewis argues that, through such media as school textbooks, the general population is being taught to believe that any statements of value are in fact meaningless as they cannot refer to anything other than subjectivity. This, he says, is a disconnection between rationality and emotion by the elimination of a training in "sentiments," which ancient philosophers described as mediating between the "spiritual" and the "animal" aspects of the human being. Already, here, we see Lewis making reference to classical conceptions of humanity. This is an initial pointer to his preference for ancient metaphysical constructs. Then, during a lightening survey of notions of "rightness" or "truth" in various cultures, Lewis slows down the pace and says:

> The Chinese also speak of a great thing (the greatest thing) called the Tao. It is the reality beyond all predicates, the abyss that was before the Creator Himself. It is nature, it is the Way, the Road. It is the Way in which the universe goes on, the Way in which things everlastingly emerge, stilly and tranquilly, into space and time. It is also the Way which every man should tread in imitation of that cosmic and supercosmic progression, conforming all activities to that great exemplar. "In ritual," say the Analects, "it is harmony with Nature that is prized." The ancient Jews likewise praise the Law as being "true."
>
> This conception in all its forms, Platonic, Aristotelian, Stoic, Christian, and Oriental alike, I shall henceforth refer to for brevity simply as "the Tao."[2]

Alarm bells went off for me when Lewis devoted this relatively long section to the description of the Confucian Tao, and then adopted that as the name for his conception of natural law. Such a law, in his account of the Tao, "is the reality beyond all predicates, the abyss that was before the Creator Himself."[3] Lewis here refers to three entries from an encyclopaedia of religion and ethics, and appears to begin by quoting a Taoist conception of the Tao, rather than the Confucian concept which is much closer to his use of the word hereafter; the Taoist concept being, in fact, rather inimical to his uses as it implies non-being, non-creativity, and emptiness rather

---

1. See, e.g. Brock, "On Whether Aquinas's *Ipsum Esse* Is Platonism"; Drever, "The Self before God?" (esp. n2); Perl, "The Presence of the Paradigm."

2. Lewis, *The Abolition of Man*, 16–17.

3. Ibid.

than the active benevolence of Confucianism. It is probable that Lewis was aware of the variant uses, and here starts with the Taoist meaning because of its more extensive ontological reach.

Whichever reference is intended, however, this specific concept is clearly non-Christian. The subordination of the Creator to the created, the presupposition of some environment called "nature," whether spiritual, mental, moral or material, into which God is then inserted, is less than the Christian conception of God as creator and sustainer of all. So the question arises, is Lewis, in adopting this expression, bringing into his argument elements that he will later regret? Is his use of the word Tao implying something about God's relationship to the universe that Lewis does not actually believe? He defines the Tao as referring to the ultimate reality "nature" "that was before the creator himself."[4]

So does he here presuppose a natural theology—a conception of a God accessible to human scrutiny, a God found in all cultures, and here merely dressed in Judeo-Christian robes for the sake of his own and his reader's comfort?

We need to beware of reading too much into Lewis's arguments, here and elsewhere, from the specific examples or illustrations he calls upon; he is not writing systematic theology—nor in fact attempting theology at all at this point. Rather his aim is to defend the notion of value and meaning in human life. He is making an apology for ethics and the place of natural law within ethics, rather than addressing the relationship of God to nature.

This distinction of purpose, by which Lewis seems to hold non-Christian views, is one which he defends in writers of antiquity, such as Boethius, in his literary work, *The Discarded Image*, saying there that "the difference between a clearly Christian and a possibly Pagan work may really be the difference between a thesis offered, so to speak, to the faculty of Philosophy and one offered to that of Divinity."[5] In other words, the purpose, the intended audience and effects, and the context of the work should be taken into consideration in judging its orthodoxy.

Why, then, does Lewis use the word Tao? Lewis is not unaware of the potential influence of specific words or patterns of thought on belief systems. "A language has its own personality; implies an outlook, reveals a mental activity, and has a resonance, not quite the same as those of any

---

4. Ibid.
5. Lewis, *The Discarded Image*, 47.

other. Not only the vocabulary—heaven can never mean quite the same as ciel—but the very shape of the syntax is sui generis."[6]

His use of the word Tao for natural law, then, should not be attributed to naivety or carelessness. It isn't as though Lewis was unaware of its non-Christian content, rather, this difference in content was unimportant for his present purpose, except so much as it prevents critics from finding that he is making, under the cloak of writing about natural law, yet another pitch for mere Christianity. In all likelihood, he is attempting here, by using a word from the "mystical east" to "sneak past watchful dragons" that would hastily jump upon any appearance of something that could be identified as a Christian apologetic. Though later he owns his theism and his Christianity, he does so in the context of an argument for "natural law" that consistently seems to subordinate individual (Christian, Platonic, or Confucian) expressions of morality to some greater conception from which they are derived and to which they refer. Later in the first chapter of *The Abolition of Man* he goes on to say that the point of the Tao for him is that there exists a common conception of reality—a form of critical realism in essence—with a moral dimension:

> What is common to [all the accounts of it] is something we cannot neglect. It is the doctrine of objective value, the belief that certain kinds of attitudes are really true and others really false, to the kind of thing the universe is and the kind of things we are. Those who know the Tao can hold that to call children delightful or old men venerable is not simply to record a psychological fact about our own parental and filial emotions at the moment, but to recognise a quality which demands a certain response from us whether we make it or not.[7]

This is a much more limited conception of Tao to that outlined so fully above; rather than a wholesale adoption of Taoist, or even Confucian, beliefs it is merely an affirmation of moral reality without any significant hint as to the content or shape of that moral reality. It deliberately does not say anything about God—it refrains even from making any claims to specific moral beliefs; merely pointing out that moral belief itself is common across cultures.

Thus, in this first chapter, Lewis does little more than introduce the idea of natural law, independently of any specific religious tradition, in

6. Ibid., 6.
7. Lewis, *The Abolition of Man*, 17.

opposition to naturalism. We do learn here, however, that we must take into account his purpose in writing before drawing conclusions from his willingness to reference other religions to support his points. We also begin to get a feel for the distinctly literary nature of his thinking.

Lewis introduced in the first chapter the recognisable figure of the modern moral "debunker." In his second chapter he has a great deal of fun debunking the debunkers, showing that attempts to discredit morality usually depend upon an implicit acceptance of some aspect of morality. This is given dramatic treatment in the first of Lewis's Cosmic Trilogy, *Out of the Silent Planet*, where the philosophising physicist, Weston, brought before the angelic guardian of Mars, is asked to justify his immoral behaviour, and is declared to have reduced all of morality to a single moral imperative, and that one not the most important.[8] Lewis had a genius for making philosophical perspectives into fictional characters, drawing out in dramatic fashion the consequences of lives lived according to the philosophies he opposed. He wasn't completely unsympathetic, however, as the revolting Weston character is replaced in the final book of the trilogy by another naturalist, the Scottish Doctor MacPhee. Macphee, however, is described as a survivor of a materialist tradition whose inherited morality kept them from the evil implied by their philosophy.[9]

Against this picture of the moral innovator, resting his case against the whole of the Tao by covertly relying upon one small strand of it, Lewis gives the picture of the poet as innovator. He does this to show that the Tao is not static or incapable of development, as his hypothetical debunking innovator might charge. He defends the Tao against charges of rigidity or traditionalism by using the illustration of change in language. Such changes can be suggested as if from the outside, by someone who, in the interests of commercial convenience or "scientific accuracy," proposes alterations to its idiom or spelling without regard for the language as a whole (I suppose that here he has the lobby for phonetic spelling in his sights). Alternatively, he says, innovations and change and development can arise from the inside of the language, by those who submit to its rules and traditions and explore and build upon already existing potentials within the language, as do poets.

In this section Lewis comes close to the borders of linguistic conceptions of religion, but he does not quite go there. His point is not that moralities (and he is, here, talking about ethical systems rather than religions

---

8. Lewis, *The Cosmic Trilogy*, 124.
9. Ibid., 560.

as such) all have their own rules and structures and unique idioms,[10] but that, like language, morality (here a global entity), is best understood and renewed from the inside by those who submit to its claims and work within its structures.

This literary analogy is interesting because it signals two things; firstly, the way in which Lewis saw ethical decisions, as with most of human life, and indeed, all of reality, as subsisting within meaningful systems, rather than as isolated and meaningless events—the random afflatus of the universe. This is consistent with a Platonic metaphysics. Secondly, that in describing the meaningfulness of any part of the universe it was only natural that he should refer to language and literature; this was, after all, his field. Though he dabbled in philosophy and theology, he was a professor of literature, and his literary interests and expertise permeated and defined a great deal of his other work.

Lewis's broader argument in this chapter invites attack at two specific points. Firstly, he puts forward an argument against "instinct" as providing sufficient justification for one human action over another. Lewis ridicules the notion that the "instinct" of caring for our offspring is a prime motivation for behaviour as we can readily observe that it is not universally or even regularly applied. We frequently act against the best interests of our progeny—for both altruistic and selfish reasons. There are, he points out, a variety of "instincts" that we can propose, and they might all be saying different things. How do we choose which is the "right" instinct? On what grounds do we accept one "instinctual" priority over another? Lewis's caricature of biological determinism could handily be addressed by, for example, Richard Dawkins's gene theory,[11] which offers a very elegant hypothesis of the role of biology in human behaviour. The weakness in Lewis's argument is limited however; biological theories of why things "are" have become better, but the strength of Lewis's argument remains. Even if gene theory can explain why we tend to do one thing rather than another, even when we seem to be acting against our (or our gene's) best interests, it cannot provide a foundation for deciding what we ought to do. It is merely a possible description of what is, not what ought to be, and Dawkins himself is at his best when he remains within those bounds. "Ought" implies values,

---

10. A concept with which he was, nevertheless, intimately aware—see above quote from, Lewis, *The Discarded Image*, 6.
11. Dawkins, *The Selfish Gene*.

and the strictly material world of the physical scientist, as understood by Dawkins and co. is value-free.

This is the core of Lewis argument against naturalist interpretations of the universe; that they render not just morality, but the whole world of meaning obsolete—and thereby destroy themselves also as he argues more completely in *Miracles*.[12]

Secondly, Lewis claims that because values of some sort must be drawn upon in order to assert particular actions as preferable or obligatory, there must be a body of natural law from which these values are drawn.[13] He then goes on to hypothesise that systems of morality are inconsistent because they are partial, and that a study of the whole will allow the perspective by which the partial can be better understood. This assumption of a greater of which the lesser is necessarily derivative strongly recalls the arguments of the seventeenth-century Cambridge neo-Platonists against the reductionism of Hobbes.[14] The weakness of the argument is that while we may accept the possibility that the existence of specific values implies a unitary and global body of values, a Tao, where is the necessity outside of Platonic-type assumptions? It would certainly be tidier if, as he claims, the universe of values is as basic to reality and as universally experienced as the sun and the sky it traverses, but where is the evidence? At best Lewis produces in his appendix a collection of sayings from various traditions under eight headings and allows his readers to notice for themselves the similarities between the various sayings. That values exist and are common currency, even among those who profess to despise them, is amply demonstrated. That they tend to cover similar areas of human life, and often say similar things about those aspects of life is also clear. That they arise from an overarching system or body of values that has reality beyond our particular systems is asserted but not shown, nor do I see how it can be shown, as any attempt to describe the "global body" of natural law must inevitably be done from within one branch of it. Where do we look to find this heavenly body if not into the particulars? And when we find global features in the particulars, how can we be sure that they are not merely our projection of that morality within which we are most comfortable?

In this mode of questioning I am adopting a stance by which I inevitably disagree with Lewis; I ask him to provide me with the specific evidence

---

12. Lewis, *Miracles* [1960].
13. Lewis, *The Abolition of Man*, 29.
14. Downie, "Cambridge Platonists."

for his general assumptions; I act, in fact, like the empiricist he opposes; I adopt an Aristotelian, naturalist perspective. But, as Lewis points out in the first chapters of Miracles, the evidence will always be understood in terms of our already-established philosophical assumptions. I say that the specific instances of his general theory can be explained in a variety of other ways, and he does not disagree, but the onus is then on me to justify the general theory by which I, in turn, explain away what he sees. He is ready and willing to justify his own perspective as one which not only accounts for observable fact, but has an internal coherence that lends it validity.

That Lewis often had recourse to a Platonic metaphysics is well-established.[15] It may be, as Andrew Walker suggests, that "Lewis's tendency to Platonise reality leads him to articulate some unfortunate and unsatisfactory theological expressions"[16] but it would be premature to judge too hastily as we discovered when investigating Lewis's use of the concept of Tao. That he is fully aware of the differences between Platonism and Christianity is illustrated by the following quote from *The Discarded Image*:

> The last, and neo-Platonic, wave of Paganism which gathered up into itself much from the proceeding waves, Aristotelian, Platonic, Stoic, and what not, came far inland and made brackish lakes which have, perhaps, never been drained. Not all Christians at all times have detected them or admitted their existence: and among those who have done so there have always been two attitudes. There was then, and is still, a Christian "left," eager to detect and anxious to banish every Pagan element; but also a Christian "right" who, like St Augustine, could find the doctrine of the Trinity foreshadowed in the Platonici,[17] or could claim triumphantly, like Justin Martyr, "Whatever things have been well said by all men belong to us Christians."[18]

By the end of the second chapter of *The Abolition of Man*, then, a rather literary Lewis has repudiated naturalism, demonstrating his bias towards neo-Platonic conceptions of meaning, and established that attempts to ridicule notions of value inevitably proceed from an implicit acceptance of some form of value. But there is another possibility—a complete and thorough-going rejection of values, and this he explores in the last chapter.

15. Wood, "Conflict and Convergence."
16. Andrew Walker, "Scripture, Revelation and Platonism in C. S. Lewis."
17. Augustine, "Confessions," 7.9.
18. Lewis, *The Discarded Image*, 48–49. Cf. Plato, *Apology* 2.13.

REVELATION AND NATURAL THEOLOGY

Chapter 3 is ultimately an argument against accepting a nature divorced from any transcendent meaning, as a "final determinant" of human values as it would inevitably lead to the abolition of all value other than the immediate gratification of the individual; in fact, though Lewis does not name names, he believes it would lead to Nietzsche's *Ubermensch*. We would find ourselves in the situation where all conceptions of human value have been reduced to projections by Feuerbach, phantasms by Freud, phenotypes by Dawkins, and there would be no reason for the will to power not to be the only determinant of human action; for there to be no rational restraint upon the desire for gratification.

Lewis suggests here that humanity may achieve a complete—or near enough to complete—power over nature, including human nature, and thus be in the position to determine the conditions by which human life may be lived hereafter. His concern is that in order to assume such a God-like power, we reduce everything, including human beings and human life, to "mere" nature, and see it in complete detachment from any framework that might give it meaning and value. To act thus is to diminish all of being to the extent that it not only may but must be treated as waste rock; mere space dust. This objectification of nature, and subjectification of meaning, he sees as the inherent tendency of modern science. Elsewhere he describes

> the great process of Internalisation which has turned genius from an attendant daemon into a quality of the mind. Always, century by century, item after item is transferred from the object's side of the account to the subject's. And now, in some extreme forms of Behaviourism, the subject himself is discounted as merely subjective; we only think that we think. Having eaten up everything else, he eats himself up too. And where we "go from that" is a dark question.[19]

Lewis depicts a bleak future in which there is nothing outside the individual subject to provide meaning or value; nothing extrinsic to the human individual to moderate our most basic desires. No point of reference outside the self. He finishes, however, on a hopeful note. He has "heard rumours" he says of re-evaluations of the romantic Goethe's approach to nature. He hopes for a science that

> when it explained . . . would not explain away. When it spoke of the parts it would remember the whole. While studying the *It* it would not lose what Martin Buber calls the *Thou*-situation. The

19. Ibid., 215.

analogy between the *Tao* of Man and the instincts of an animal species would mean for it a new light cast on the unknown thing, Instinct, by the inly known reality of conscience and not a reduction of conscience to the category of Instinct. Its followers would not be free with the words only and merely.[20]

Lewis concludes with the observation "If you see through everything, then everything is transparent. But a wholly transparent world is an invisible world. To 'see through' all things is the same as not to see."

What might these rumours have been, to which Lewis refers? One candidate is a physical scientist, a contemporary of Lewis, who was doing precisely what Lewis here calls for. Michael Polanyi also argued against reductionism in the sciences and made a strong case for accrediting non-empirical knowledge, what Lewis described as the "inly known reality" and Polanyi called "personal knowledge." As I have previously commented,[21] however, Polanyi's epistemological vision falls a little short of a truly Christian understanding, at precisely the hurdle Lewis refers to above; while Polanyi does attempt to see the part in terms of the whole, he nowhere moves beyond a naturalistic understanding of the universe. That is, he sees meaning as emergent rather than as truly personal. He does not propose an "I-Thou" relationship for the human observer of reality, but an "I-it" relationship. At that time I suggested that a better, though significantly less developed, model for epistemology might be found in Blaise Pascal whose overwhelming awareness of the significance of the hidden God meant that his explorations of the universe take on a significantly humbler character; more that of the worshipper than the *Ubermensch*. Lewis, similarly, presupposes a reality in which the personal character of human knowledge is acknowledged, but so also is the possibility—for Lewis, the certainty—of the Person whose primacy determines every other aspect of reality. Thus, emergent meaning is not adequate for Lewis, as he makes clear in *Miracles*.[22] He continues to prefer a Platonic over an Aristotelian epistemology.

Thus we have, in *The Abolition of Man*, a plea against deterministic, reductionist science to become the final arbiter of value. The attempts to cut down to mere nature the great tree of the Tao are frequently, as Lewis points out in his second chapter, scuttled by the fact that the chopper takes a stand

---

20. Lewis, *The Abolition of Man*, 54.

21. In a paper presented to the Polanyi Consortium, Tyndale-Carey Postgraduate School, 2008.

22. Lewis, *Miracles* [1960], 34.

REVELATION AND NATURAL THEOLOGY

upon some branch of the Tao whilst swinging the axe. But there remain those who simply declare, against Plato, Pascal, and Polanyi, the meaninglessness of human life observed as a simple natural phenomenon. Lewis protests that if all that is, is merely dust and accident, then values do not have validity. *The Abolition of Man* is his argument for the rationality of morality and the necessity for it if we are to live as real human beings. But whilst he has adequately described morality as a universal human trait, and consistently implies a neo-Platonist metaphysics, he has not explicitly anchored it into a coherent vision of reality.

Just such a vision, however, is offered in an address from the same era. In the essay "Transposition" Lewis sketches an epistemological framework that allows for a comprehensive view of the natural world and a revaluing of all that is in the light of a transcendent reality. In *The Abolition of Man*, Lewis focuses upon "values," upon finding meanings that privilege one human action over another, meaning that naturally suggests an "ought." In "Transposition," he addresses the more basic question of how it is possible to sustain any meaning at all in the face of the naturalist reduction of all phenomena to the inane. Here he puts his metaphysics in full view and demonstrates its utility not just for providing a framework by which we may secure meaning itself, but by which we may approach the central Christian mystery: the incarnation.

TRANSPOSITION

In "Transposition" Lewis begins with the difficulty of ascribing meaning to phenomena; starting with glossolalia, he then moves quickly to the pseudo-erotic imagery of the mystics, and thence to the physical sensations that accompany both pleasurable and deeply unpleasant emotional responses. As he does he presents his question thus:

> Our problem is that of the obvious continuity between things which are admittedly natural and things which, it is claimed, are spiritual; the reappearance in what professes to be our supernatural life of all the same old elements which make up our natural life and (it would seem) of no others. If we have really been visited by a revelation from beyond Nature, is it not very surprising that an Apocalypse can furnish heaven with nothing more than selections from terrestrial experience (crowns, thrones, and music) that devotion can find no language but that of human lovers, and that the rite whereby Christians enact a mystical union should turn out to

49

be only the old, familiar act of eating and drinking? And you may add that the very same problem breaks out on a lower level, not only between spiritual and natural, but also between higher and lower levels of the natural life. Hence cynics very plausibly challenge our civilised conception of the difference between love and lust by pointing out that when all is said and done they usually end in what is, physically, the same act. They similarly challenge the difference between justice and revenge on the ground that what finally happens to the criminal may be the same. And in all these cases, let us admit that the cynics have a good prima facie case.[23]

Here Lewis is once again dealing with reductionist or materialist debunkers of meaning. He responds by showing how it is reasonable and normal for interpretations of the same material details to vary significantly in the weightiness of their meanings.

It is worth noting that while at this point he proposes a continuity between the spiritual and the natural, he argues for this continuity in terms of the human experience of what is spiritual and what is natural; in other words he is not necessarily saying that they are ontologically continuous, but that the human experience—or at least the human expression of both natural and spiritual phenomena—is continuous. He is talking here in terms of epistemology rather than ontology. This is not necessarily the *analogia entis* so much as an *analogia intellectus* or *analogia ratio*. In fact Lewis seems to imply, by talking of a revelation from beyond nature, the transcendence of the Divine.

There is, however, as he notes, a correspondence between our spiritual and our natural experience, and his first step in establishing the rationality of this correspondence is to show, on a purely naturalist level, how physical sensations can have a variety of meanings dependent upon context and personal evaluations of the sensation. The feeling of "being a little sick" in the stomach, can be associated with motion sickness, with musical delight, with love-sickness! Thus Lewis establishes his basic premise; that individual phenomena can justifiably bear a range of interpretations within a naturalistic framework. This is so, he says, because we have a wide range of emotions, but a very limited range of actual sensations available to us. Therefore the same sensations must do double-duty in accompanying and embodying a wide range of emotional experiences.

---

23. Lewis, *Transposition, and Other Addresses*, 69–70.

Lewis then expands on this phenomenon of what he comes to call "Transposition" with a range of examples: he points to a limited number of vowel symbols (five) used to represent twenty-two vowel sounds; the ability to represent an entire orchestral score as a score for the piano alone; and a limited range of two-dimensional shapes and shades on paper being interpreted as a whole range of three-dimensional figures with a variety of qualities of light.

It is from the musical example that he takes the word "transposition," and it is here that he most compellingly reasserts the necessity of adopting a broad philosophical framework—a transcendent perspective—from which to interpret individual phenomena. He points out that one who has heard (or at least read) the entire orchestral score, can read into the piano score the same range of sounds and recall the much richer experience. One who has only ever had acquaintance with the piano score—and has no inkling of a possible orchestral score—cannot interpret the piano score in that way. Similarly, a two-dimensional creature could not, from experience, grant the reality of the two-dimensional representation of a three-dimensional reality to be anything other than two-dimensional figures. The lower range is given meaning by the higher, the higher cannot be interpreted by the lower. To restrict our understanding to bare "facts" is to restrict ourselves to relative meaninglessness. We must interpret the facts according to some higher, more complex scheme than they themselves communicate or be left with simplistic tautologies of the most meaningless kind, much like those scorned by J. R. R. Tolkien in the opening lines of his poem "Mythopoeia."[24]

Both men came to agree that naturalism left us with nothing more than the inane. Against such meaninglessness Tolkien here points to the nature of speech itself as a means of comprehending that our relationship with the world of which we are part is necessarily a meaning-making experience. Lewis, with his concept of transposition, offers something similar, but in a more general sense. He sees a broadly operating epistemological pattern whereby the lesser must be interpreted in the light of the greater. Thus he defends the necessity, in epistemology, as he has previously done in morality, of understanding particular phenomena in terms of broader, higher, deeper, more complex beliefs, rather than in terms of lesser, more

---

24. J. R. R. Tolkien, *Tree and Leaf Including the Poem Mythopoeia*. This poem has a significant place in Lewis's intellectual history, as it is a record by Tolkien of a conversation one night that later proved to be a turning point in Lewis's acceptance of the Christian faith.

limited, "facts." Again, a Platonic metaphysics seems to be in operation here.

This then leads him to some interesting observations on the nature of symbolism. He describes a symbol as something that has no inherent relationship to that which it points; thus the letter "a" has no necessary connection to the sounds that we associate with it, nor does a crochet on a stave necessarily communicate anything about music; these symbols have their meanings entirely by convention. This is one form of "transposition," whereby marks on paper attain meaning beyond themselves by virtue of symbolic operations. The relationship is arbitrary and imposed by meaning-making creatures. In such instances of the imposition of meaning by humans on the universe, there is no evidence of inherent meaning; we may be merely deluding ourselves.

There are other forms of transposition, however, that are not "symbolic" in this way, and he uses the example of a picture. A picture becomes what it means to us, not entirely through convention, but by virtue of the more complex operations by which we also know that which it represents. Both the picture and the landscape it represents are visible to us by virtue of light shining on each. The picture, in fact, is a visible object in the world of visible objects that it depicts. It is an instance of that which it represents. As Lewis says: "The sunlight in a picture is therefore not related to real sunlight simply as written words are to spoken. It is a sign, but also something more than a sign: . . . because in it the thing signified is really in a certain mode present. If I had to name the relation I should call it not symbolical but sacramental."[25]

This leads Lewis back to his starting point—the difficulty for descriptions of spiritual realities that they rely upon words and concepts that do not necessarily have spiritual meanings—the old problem of analogy. His argument, then, is that it is inevitable that we, who are lower, must rely upon words and meanings and objects and phenomena drawn from and part of the world of nature to understand and express what is transcendently true; what is of God. This is primarily an epistemological argument, but when he begins to talk of the sacramental, Lewis begins to cross over into ontology. The picture of the sun communicates "sun" because it reflects actual light. Light really is present in this picture of light. Physical sensations do not merely "mean" emotions by arbitrary assignation, but are the emotion in its physical aspect by association with emotional meaning. They "incarnate"

25. Lewis, "Transposition," 15.

the emotion. This leads Lewis to say—in a qualified manner as he was quite aware that he was, if not swimming beyond his depth then at least paddling in someone else's pool—that there is here "a real analogy"[26] between what he has described as transposition and the incarnation.

In *The Abolition of Man*, Lewis wrote as a moralist, not necessarily as a Christian. He appealed to rationality and freedom as opposed to meaninglessness and slavery. In "Transposition" the Platonic metaphysics there implied becomes explicit in all but name; here we seem to have the "Ideal" finding expression in natural forms. Does Lewis therefore assume an ontological continuity between the natural and the spiritual, the human and the divine? Does his *analogia intellectus* become an *analogia entis* at this point? In attempting to answer this question, we must look again beyond this essay. Like *The Abolition of Man*, "Transposition" is a partial and polemical outline, presented originally as a single lecture. I turn now to *Miracles*.

MIRACLES

In the early chapters of *Miracles* we are given a fuller expression of Lewis's understanding of the relationship between the transcendent, called there the "super-natural" and the "natural." Lewis there provides for rationality itself the same argument provided in *The Abolition of Man* for morality. In doing so he claims that rationality is not "natural" in the sense that it could not have "emerged" from purely natural processes; there must have been a higher, ordering event or process by which rational thought came to occur in human beings. He thus describes rationality as "supernatural," though a better word may have been "transcendent." Certainly he sees rationality as trans-natural. This becomes for him, as for Augustine, the point of connection between the divine and the natural, creator and created. We can see here that there is, in fact, an analogia entis, an assertion of absolute continuity between the being of humanity and the being of God. It is rationality in God that has led to rationality in humanity. Rationality in humanity, on a purely logical basis, then becomes a reason for finding rationality in the divine. God is thus disclosed not through revelation, but through anthropology; precisely the outcome feared by Barth.

It is certainly possible to read Lewis as making the above argument for the rationality of belief in God, but this is not his characteristic argument, nor is it central to the model of reality which, we begin to see, exists in

26. Ibid., 19.

his mind. Lewis does not argue from the ground up, but from the heavens down—he is traditionally "Platonic" in that respect. Therefore he is quite clear that though pagan myths may point towards Christ, and do so as evidence of God's grace rather than as evidence of man's perversion, that evidence can only be recognised as such in the light of Christ himself. The piano score cannot be made to represent the whole orchestra unless the orchestral music is known. An *analogia entis* does not work in a Platonic world, only in an Aristotelian. Barth's shafts pass Lewis by.

Nor may we charge Lewis with that other bogey of post-liberal or Neo-orthodox theology, that of foundationalism, for his use of Platonism. Lewis knows, preaches, and bows delightedly before the sovereignty of God. Who has not used occasionally the phrase "He's not a tame Lion"? That all human thought is provisional and inadequate is something he's quite familiar with. In the epilogue of *The Discarded Image* he acknowledges his appreciation of the mediaeval model of reality, then goes on to say:

> I hope no one will think I am recommending a return to the Medieval Model. I am only suggesting considerations that may induce us to regard all Models in the right way, respecting each and idolising none. . . . We can no longer dismiss the change in models as a simple progress from error to truth. No Model is a catalogue of ultimate realities, and none is a mere fantasy. Each is a serious attempt to get in all the phenomena known at a given period, and each succeeds in getting in a great many.[27]

Lewis, then, is no foundationalist, putting Plato or any other conception of reality before Nature or God—though he notes carefully that the reality we find depends on the questions we ask, and the questions we ask depend on the perspective we bring to the task. So why does Lewis allow his Platonic preferences to lead him to what Walker described as "unfortunate and unsatisfactory theological expressions." Primarily because Lewis is not a theologian—this both limits him and gives him freedom. He has here been writing as a popular apologist in a highly polemical context, of which he says: "One is fighting on at least two fronts. When one is among Pantheists one must emphasise the distinctness, and relative independence, of the creatures. Among Deists—or perhaps in Woolwich, if the laity there really think God is to be sought in the sky—one must emphasise the divine presence in my neighbour, my dog, my cabbage-patch."[28]

27. Lewis, *The Discarded Image*, 222.
28. Lewis, *Prayer: Letters to Malcolm*, 99.

Just such a reference is probably precisely what Andrew Walker has in mind as an "unfortunate and unsatisfactory theological expression." But Walker mistakes his genres. Lewis is not attempting a balanced and systematic theological, ontological, or epistemological exposition. He is attempting to persuade. He is deliberately unbalanced so as to make his mark on a particular target. He does have and rely upon ontology and epistemology, and the literary, neo-Platonic nature of these is well illustrated, but so is their provisional place in his thought. If there is anything fixed and solid in Lewis's thinking, it is theological; it is what God has done in Jesus Christ. He takes profoundly seriously the miracle of the incarnation, describing it as the central act of God in the world[29] which sets the pattern for every other such act. God relates to the world via incarnation, and neo-Platonism provides a means for getting some grasp on what that might mean. Among other things, it means that even in our thought life, in our earth-bound ideas and understandings, there is also the possibility—even the probability—of God's very truth. Thus, ideas like neo-Platonism, can, in the light of Christ, be found to foreshadow Christian truth and reality. Human ideological constructs, no less than other human bodies, may become fit dwelling places for and very temples of, the Spirit of Truth. That Lewis finds evidence of God in nature, of Christ in myths of Corn-kings, of a "sacrament" of Christian truth truly existing in all of life, is not because Lewis adopts a classical monism, seeing all of being as completely continuous, but because he is Christianly incarnational. As Ralph Wood puts it, "Lewis was a Platonist Christian and not a Christian Platonist."[30] In his last book, published posthumously, Lewis writes,

> All creatures, from the angel to the atom, are other than God; with an otherness to which there is no parallel: incommensurable. The very word "to be" cannot be applied to Him and to them in exactly the same sense. But also, no creature is other than He is in the same way in which it is other than all the rest. He is in it as they can never be in one another. In each of them as the ground and root and continual supply of its reality....
>
> Therefore of each creature we can say, "This also is Thou: neither is this Thou."[31]

---

29. Lewis, *Miracles* [1960], 112.
30. Wood, "Conflict and Convergence," 9.
31. Lewis, *Prayer: Letters to Malcolm*, 98–99.

Thus, Lewis affirms a central paradox of all Christian theology: that God is completely hidden and beyond all human knowledge, and that God has so revealed himself to us that we are guilty if we do not acknowledge him with thanksgiving at every sunrise and leaf fall.

4

C. S. Lewis's Argument against Naturalism

JOHN OWENS

THE VIEW THAT HUMAN reasoning might be a simple product of natural causes, coming into existence in the same sort of way as does a stalactite or a volcanic eruption or an avalanche, has long exercised a hold on the philosophical imagination. C. S. Lewis calls the view "naturalism," and believes that it is fundamentally misguided, and even self-contradictory. His first attack on naturalism, in a book published in 1947, dispatches it briskly, in a chapter of a few pages.[1] He holds that naturalism destroys the possibility of valid reasoning, and therefore self-destructs, given that it is a product of reasoning. The problem is to show exactly why reasoning is destroyed or impossible, if the naturalist explanation is allowed. Most of us would agree that some natural causes destroy the validity of reasoning, as when an emotional prejudice interferes with the rational development of an argument. If an argument is shown to depend on such a thing, it is dismissed as invalid. But there might be other kinds of natural causes (which Lewis's critic Elizabeth Anscombe calls "non-rational"[2]) that produce something valid and true. We are familiar with mechanical calculators which work

---

1. Lewis, *Miracles*, 1947. For the revised version of the argument, see Lewis, *Miracles*, 1960.

2. Anscombe, "C. S. Lewis on 'Naturalism,'" 226.

by natural process, and which use informational premises to produce true conclusions. What if the human brain works in more or less the same way, so that what we call valid thought or reasoning is ultimately the product of a certain sort of complex natural process? Naturalism appeals to those who regard contemporary science as a paradigm of explanation. Anscombe more or less defines naturalism in this way, as the view that "all human behaviour, including thought, could be accounted for by scientific causal laws."[3] She later glosses this definition as the position that "causal laws could be discovered which could be successfully applied to all human behaviour, including thought."[4]

Lewis and Anscombe had a celebrated debate in February 1948 that caused Lewis to revise some of his views.[5] But he remained unimpressed by naturalist accounts, and insisted to the end that a reasoning process has to include "a moment of insight" that transcends mere natural process, if it is to be regarded as valid. A calculating machine might arrive at results that are true, but it includes no moment of insight among its premises. Its activity is therefore deficient in an important respect. It is not enough for our thought processes to arrive at results that just happen to be correct. The results need to be produced by activity of a certain quality, described as "insight" or "actual reasoning," if they are to have any worth. Anscombe notes this point during the debate, remarking that Lewis is probably more interested in the question of whether someone actually reasoned than in the question of whether the reasoning merely led to a true conclusion or not.[6] In my view, Lewis is on to something deep here. But at the time of the argument with Anscombe, there is no sign that he appreciated what it was. Anscombe notes that at the time of the debate, neither of them appreciated the depth of the issue that was in question,[7] and Lewis himself acknowledged that the topic of the debate was not really "validity."[8] I think that the real topic of the debate is the self-transcendence of knowledge, the fact that it is knowledge of the other, and that this has implications for the status of the human being. In his later writings Lewis shows a profound appreciation

3. Ibid.
4. Ibid., 229.
5. For an account of the debate, see Walter Hooper, "Oxford's Bonny Fighter." For a more recent discussion see Reppert, *C. S. Lewis's Dangerous Idea*.
6. Anscombe, "C. S. Lewis on 'Naturalism,'" 228.
7. Anscombe, *Metaphysics and the Philosophy of Mind*, 2:x.
8. Cf. Anscombe, "C. S. Lewis on 'Naturalism,'" 231.

of such things, for all that he never seems to connect his later discussions with the debate on naturalism.

Lewis's insistence that valid reasoning must include a moment of insight, shows that his argument differs from a similar argument put forward by Alvin Plantinga, which has attracted a good deal of attention, including a book of critical responses.[9] Plantinga criticizes an evolutionary form of the naturalist position, which holds that our beliefs might have developed through natural processes, with evolutionary selection weeding out those which are false, leaving us with beliefs that are largely true. Lewis himself has a brief discussion of this position.[10] So the blind evolutionary drive of a species towards survival enables it to develop beliefs about the world which happen to be true. In arguing against this view, Plantinga points out that for every true belief that helps us operate in the world, there are multitudes of equally effective false beliefs. If I hold the true belief that tigers are dangerous, and therefore run away when I see a tiger, this helps me to survive. But as Plantinga points out (in a rather odd example), a person who holds that tigers are friendly, but who thinks that the best way to pet a tiger is to run away from it, does just as well.[11] These false beliefs are equally effective in ensuring my survival. Given that the number of possible false beliefs far outweighs the single true belief which applies in a particular case, it is much more likely that an evolutionary process produce beliefs which are false rather than beliefs which are true. While at times Lewis gives the impression of considering this form of the argument favourably,[12] it seems in fact far removed from the position he wants to defend. The difference is shown by the fact that within the terms of Plantinga's argument, if it happened that natural processes arrived at true conclusions in a reliable manner, then naturalism would be satisfactory. It seems clear that Lewis wants to put forward a far stronger argument than this. He is against the naturalist position even if it happens that in some or many cases, a natural process produces true conclusions. Again and again, he says that it is not satisfactory if beliefs just happen to correspond to the state of the world. Why exactly this is not satisfactory, and what it is that Lewis has stumbled upon here, is the topic of this paper.

---

9. Plantinga, "Is Naturalism Irrational?" and "Naturalism Defeated?"
10. Lewis, *Miracles*, 22–23.
11. Plantinga, "Is Naturalism Irrational?," 225.
12. Lewis, *Miracles*, 22.

A MYTH RETOLD

What is the precise difference between someone whose beliefs just happen to correspond to the world, and someone who holds true beliefs in the fuller sense which Lewis wants to defend, where the beliefs result from "a moment of insight"? The difference emerges if we think of examples of beliefs which just happen to correspond to reality. We know of sophisticated missiles which carry a map of the terrain over which they are to be deployed. The map enables them to manoeuvre effectively in relation to the terrain, so that they might navigate around geographical features which would otherwise block their progress. Naturalist philosophers tend to see the human mind as operating more or less like this (with the difference that the human mind has not been programmed by an intelligence). Its knowledge goes back to a set of guides in the head, which have been formed by causal processes, and which control its behaviour. The workings of these processes might even deliver certain experiences as well. The more accurately the guide can represent what is really there, the more effective is the action that follows. The philosopher Patricia Churchland holds that such maps have arisen through natural selection, and that it is a great advantage for survival if a map actually matches the contours of the reality that it depicts.[13] But it is clear that while there is a sense in which such minds reach true conclusions about the external world, they just happen to have come to these. They would happily have embraced other conclusions, if such conclusions enabled them to operate equally effectively in the world.

One of the most striking things about this sort of theory (which carries a nominalist frame of mind to an extreme), is that it does not allow for relations between things. While it sees the mind as happening to correspond to the way things are, the mind does not does not relate itself in any sense to the world it represents. For the naturalist view, everything in the world is just itself, and does not reach outside itself in any way. The point is shown in the fact that while there may be a correspondence between picture and world, the correspondence is only ever registered as such from outside the picture. This view has turned up in the history of philosophy in the kind of system proposed by Leibniz, where the perceptions of the individual mind are limited to the interior of the mind, and do not reach beyond themselves to the real world which they represent. It happens that human intentional states often correspond with what is really the case, or at least, to the perceptions of other monads about what is the case. In Leibniz's

---

13. Churchland, *Brain-Wise*, 302–8, 364. The use of the "map" analogy is quite common. See for example Ramsey, "Naturalism Defended," 18.

system God has arranged such a set of coincidences, and God also registers the correspondence of the mind's perceptions to things beyond them. But the human mind itself does not relate itself directly to anything outside it in this way. As Leibniz famously says, the monads have no windows through which anything could enter or depart.[14] A philosopher of a different stamp, who shares important premises with Leibniz—David Hume—sums it up with his usual clarity and succinctness: "We never really advance a step beyond ourselves."[15]

Naturalism holds the nominalist premise, that everything is simply itself, and that while some things may correspond to other things in the world, they do not relate themselves to the other things. In the naturalist view, no event reaches outside itself to any other event. Lewis sums it up in referring critically to the view that the workings of the mind are straightforward events: "[e]vents in general are not 'about' anything and cannot be true or false."[16] If, as the naturalist view has it, our convictions are simply events like this, they are "a fact about us—like the colour of our hair."[17] For a fact to become a representation, we have to introduce a relation into things, namely the eye of an observer who has an interest in knowing how the image in the mind corresponds to the object in the world. Such an observer must be really related to the world, if the scheme is to work. Nor is it enough that the beliefs of the observer simply happen to mirror the state of the world in their turn. If it is like this, then the problem is simply pushed back a level, and we need a new observer at a higher level who can note the correlation between the lower observer's beliefs and the world, and grasp it in the sort of relation traditionally called "knowledge."

Naturalists want to argue that there is no problem with a world in which everything remains within its own limits, and where the only sort of "knowledge" consists of brain states which happen to be correlates of states of affairs in the world. The eye of the technician that correlates the map of the missile to the outside terrain works in much the same way as does the missile itself. So the observer who has an interest in the outcome is viewed in turn as a configuration of materials and forces, that act in a way which is naturalistically explainable. Anyone who considers this argument quickly realizes that whatever is thrown at the naturalist position, it

14. Leibniz, "The Monadology," 7 , 643.
15. Hume, *A Treatise of Human Nature*, 1.2.67.
16. Lewis, *Miracles*, 21.
17. Ibid., 109.

will always have an answer. Even validity and truth can be redefined to fit the scheme, so that they are integrated into a naturalist account. What we call "moments of insight" might be just correlations which help us make our way in the world, delivering certain conscious experiences at the same time, including a sense that we are seeing directly into the outside world.

Lewis insists that the naturalist account is not enough, and that a recognition of truth is needed, which proceeds from a real relation of knower to reality. As he says, a premise has to cause a conclusion "by being seen to be, a ground for it."[18] An act of knowing must be determined "in a sense, solely by what is known." "[W]e must know it to be thus solely because it is thus."[19] The "positive character" of the act of knowledge "must be determined by the truth it knows."[20] He sees a contrast between two sorts of causal action. With the first, the world produces certain effects in us, whether we like it or not, including our beliefs. With the second, there is a different sort of causality, where "the truth" of the matter does the causing, and where we see ourselves as having "insight" into a state of affairs. Lewis expresses this as the difference between "responses to stimuli" (things like pains),[21] and acts of knowledge which are "insights into, or knowings of, something other than themselves."[22] But this second kind of action, which Lewis defends as leading to knowledge of the truth, needs clarification. I know what it is for the wind to act on me. It is not immediately clear what it means for "the truth" of a situation to act on me. Nor is it clear why this second kind of relation matters so much, given that we can imagine our knowledge working more or less effectively without it.

If it is not enough that conclusions just happen to be true, then the relation between mind and knower must include some sort of necessity. It is not however clear what could be meant by "necessity" here. Obviously it does not refer to the physical necessities of natural causal action, as this sort of necessity precisely characterizes the naturalist view, where the world's causal action builds up a set of beliefs without any regard for whether they are true or not. Lewis indicates a possible different meaning of "necessity" in a much later work, *The Abolition of Man*, which begins with a discussion of those for whom the remark of a tourist about Niagara Falls is taken to

18. Ibid., 21.
19. Ibid., 22.
20. Ibid.
21. Ibid., 23.
22. Ibid., 21.

be "a remark about his own feelings,"[23] in other words an articulation of a causal impact which the world has made on the tourist. Lewis contrasts this understanding with a more traditional one, where reality itself seems to call forth a particular response from us, so that we are faced with a kind of moral compulsion, feeling that we should give the response which reality not only causes, but which it also deserves, in that the response describes it accurately as it is. One of his examples is the call to see children as "delightful" or old men as "venerable."[24] Here there is a peculiar sort of "necessity" in question, which does not work of its own accord, independently of subjectivity, but which operates as a kind of call for recognition. Humans are not forced in any physical sense to grant such recognition. The call can however haunt them if they refuse it, and even pursue them until they give in. At least the "good" person experiences such a call in this way. Lewis opposes this understanding to the naturalist view, which sees our beliefs as imposed on us by natural process, and where the relation between beliefs and world is just one of chance.

Such descriptions of human moral experience are common enough. What is less common is the point that they show us how we come in the first place to the idea of "reality," getting beyond the shadowy objects of the naturalist view, which are essentially projections out of a causal impact of an object on our knowledge apparatus. The moral call solicits an acknowledgment of what reality somehow deserves. To come to something like this is to get beyond the distortions introduced by our own interests, which encourage us to limit our view of the thing to its significance for us. When describing this transition, Lewis insists that valid reasoning does not simply "record a psychological fact about our . . . emotions at the moment."[25] It takes account of the fact that reality can merit certain responses, as opposed to just arousing or producing them.[26] The "good" person is precisely the one who has learned the right habitual reactions to the reality of things, so that they cannot help but rejoice in the presence of what is good, and recoil from what is bad. Lewis sees the older Western tradition of education, established by Plato and Aristotle, as trying to bring its students to the point where such reactions are easy and natural.[27]

23. Lewis, *The Abolition of Man*, 7–8.
24. Ibid., 17.
25. Ibid.
26. Ibid., 15.
27. Ibid., 15–16.

Lewis offers a striking example of what is meant in the book *A Grief Observed*. The book begins with a state of mind that is basically the result of causal impact, something which lends itself to description within a naturalist schema. It describes the passage towards a different state of mind, where the subject becomes really related to something outside him. It is a moral journey, one which calls up all the reserves of patient endurance which a human being can muster. The causal impact is of course the death of Lewis's wife Joy. The book starts with his living through the effect of this, and it gives a harrowing account of the states of mind which the bereavement induces. Lewis's description of these caused states, made from a later point when he has passed beyond them, employs some significant expressions. The states of mind are "a self-hypnosis induced by my own prayers,"[28] a "pipe-dream" or a "phantom,"[29] "dreams" and "houses of cards."[30] Such terms are classic expressions of perceptions which are simply causal products. In the history of philosophy, they have been summed up in the image of the "dream." While a dream is a type of awareness, in that it presents itself as an object of the mind, the only connection it has with the world is that it is ultimately caused by the world. It has no direct representative relation to the world, but remains a mere perception, leaving me immersed in my own states, even as it appears to take me beyond them. It is of course possible that the content of my dream happens to correspond to what is the case in the world. I might start to dream of rain precisely at the moment when rain starts beating on the roof, and the sound of the rain might even have caused me to have the dream. But while the dream is caused by the rain, it is not a representation of it in any strong sense. The dream happens to correspond to reality, but does not relate itself to reality, remaining a private possession of a monad without windows. It does not attain the "real" world which we share with others, but remains a private possession, where in Hume's phrase "we never really advance a step beyond ourselves." The world remains essentially private, and there is no relation to a world which we might share with others. The philosopher Heraclitus has a classic expression of this from the beginnings of Western philosophy: "The world of the waking is one and shared, but the sleeping turn aside each into his private world."[31]

28. Lewis, *A Grief Observed*, 11.
29. Ibid.
30. Ibid., 33–35.
31. Heraclitus, "Fragments," 31.

In *A Grief Observed*, Lewis describes the journey of a human being away from such dreams, which are projections which result from the impact of feelings of loss, to an awareness of reality as it is. A large part of this journey consists of his overcoming a state where, as at least appears in hindsight, his mind is dominated by the mere effects of what has happened to him, to arrive at a point where he can see the reality of things. It is only when he has in a sense got past the effect of Joy's loss, that he can come to appreciate the reality of what he has lost. There is a place in the middle of the book where he says "suddenly at the very moment when, so far, I mourned Helen least, I remembered her best. . . . To say it was like a meeting, would be going too far."[32] He has come to a point where he finds Joy "obstinately real," so that he is beyond the place where she is just a projection out of his own interior state. This is to come to a reality whose significance is independent, and whose worth does not come down to Lewis's likes or dislikes.[33] He puts this remark in the context of one of his favourite themes, that reality is iconoclastic, always letting us know that it is more than just the object of our thoughts. The one you love, in this life, "incessantly triumphs over your mere idea of her. And you want her to."[34] It is striking that among other things, this is a moral journey. At the beginning of the book, he is tempted to give in to the dream, and produce a view of his situation which is a product of the causal influence which the situation exercises. It is a moral achievement not to give in to this, but to come to acknowledge the reality of it all.

It is striking that there is no obvious phenomenological difference, no quality of the object before the mind (like Hume's attempted criterion of "force and liveliness"[35]), that might distinguish the real Joy from the dream-image which stood for her at the start of the book, and was a kind of fabrication of Lewis's grief. We do not seem to encounter the reality of something at this level. Even when someone addresses us in some way, we are never forced to acknowledge their reality, and can always stand off and register their actions simply as "data," to which we supply a hypothesis. The life of another does not force itself on us. As some philosophers have noted, we can regard others as simulations or machines or zombies, if we want. Lewis's journey from projections towards reality seems connected with the

32. Lewis, *A Grief Observed*, 37.
33. Ibid., 42.
34. Ibid., 52.
35. Hume, *A Treatise of Human Nature*, 1.1.1.1.

fact that by the end of the journey Joy faces him again. She has moved from being an image that is a frozen product of grief, to the point where she appears before Lewis again with a life of her own, that somehow faces him directly, and challenges the illusions that his grief has brought. She comes before him again with a life of her own. Lewis has a striking experience of this, which he describes as "[j]ust the impression of her mind momentarily facing my own."[36] Most of us can relate to what Lewis is trying to say, and yet it is mysterious what more such an experience brings, that was not there before. The detailed content of such an image is no more than it was when Joy was just a frozen product of Lewis's mind. In both cases there is a registration and processing of stuff, colours and movements, the sorts of things a sensor, whose operation can be naturalistically explained, can pick up and process. At this level, where content is simply "registered," it does not matter whether the object is real or not. Our dealings with the world can be described in a perfectly good naturalist manner, and we can imagine a well-programmed machine that would perform them just as efficiently.

But the good person never remains just at this level. Starting with our experience of other persons, we acknowledge their reality, seeing them as having a significance beyond just the significance they have for us. Part of Lewis's overall project is to highlight the strangeness of this move, however basic it is to the life of humans. The move to the reality of the other oddly transcends anything we could consider in the way of interactions between material things, the kind of model on which the naturalist hypothesis tries to construct its view of knowledge.

This peculiar relation that discovers the reality of the other is of a different order from the registration of objective content. When we realize this, the fundamental mysteriousness of human relational life comes into focus, along with the possibility of an openness to the divine. Christians believe that the first principle of the world's changing manifold is a "someone," and not "something," so that reality bears in on us ultimately as someone who stands over against us, with the force of a challenge. While this transcends other relations which the human being takes up, it is not completely different from the way in which we come to acknowledge the reality of other living things, especially other human beings. Lewis has a vivid description of his coming to this awareness in a religious sense towards the end of *Surprised by Joy*, as he comes to the decisive moment of his reconversion and return to Christianity. He is in the bus going up Headington

---

36. Lewis, *A Grief Observed*, 57.

Hill, and becomes aware of the ultimate reality as bearing in on him. It is as though he is confronted by a person who asks acknowledgment, although there is no person present to him in any usual sense. He says "[w]ithout words and (I think) almost without images, a fact about myself was somehow presented to me. I became aware that I was holding something at bay, or shutting something out."[37] He felt he was wearing stiff clothing, or a suit of armour, like a lobster, that he could keep on or not. Eventually, he chose to take it off.

While this was a free choice, it was one where it did not really seem possible to do the opposite. To refuse the response would feel like wilfulness on our part, as though we were keeping something out, and refusing an open stance towards the world. When this sort of choice comes at us at the highest, purest level, it is the religious choice. I think if helps if we see that the religious experience of being addressed by reality in some way, is not a strange exception to our normal ontology, but is in fact an example of the norm, the kind of thing we do whenever we come to an appreciation of reality that gets beyond a mere projection of objects. This well sums up what is needed to approach reality as reality, a kind of moral acknowledgment which we have the power to withhold, but which every good person makes to some degree. This would imply that the religious move is rather more in continuity with other everyday moves of human beings, than a secular frame of mind would like to think. The sort of response in question is what a machine cannot do, however much it can simulate the various registrations and reactions that accompany such a response.

Lewis first addresses these questions in a book on miracles. He wants his readers to consider the possibility that God sometimes acts directly in the world, intervening from outside its normal causal workings. To make this plausible, he has to break the spell of the naturalist view, which insists that natural causes sufficiently explain whatever happens, so that there is never any need to appeal outside the spatio-temporal order. Lewis's strategy is to show that not only is nature open to being influenced from outside, but that this happens quite often. Every time we attempt a piece of reasoning, something from outside nature (what Lewis calls, rather misleadingly, "the supernatural") is brought to bear on nature, so that even the everyday use of reason cannot be thought of as just part of the natural world. To contemporary ears, this can seem an odd position to hold. But it relates to the older Western tradition, and is captured in Aristotle's famous, quixotic comment

---

37. Lewis, *Surprised by Joy*, 179.

A MYTH RETOLD

that "[i]t remains, then, that Reason alone enters in, as an additional factor, from outside, and that it alone is divine."[38] Lewis sees that if he can show that the natural order is susceptible to frequent causal action from outside like this, then a divine agent's occasional action within this order will seem less strange.

Lewis tries to argue that naturalism, the view that everything, including our knowledge, works by mere causal process, is incompatible with rational thinking. But his argument implicitly shows that it is incompatible with a good deal more than this, and that in the end, it excludes any real relation to reality. This means that the naturalist view cannot accommodate life-processes at all, but inevitably sees them in such a way that they are reduced to simulations. Nor can it accommodate the strange relation to others that is knowledge, however well it mimics the material processes that accompany it. In a naturalist view we are only ever shadows for one another, experienced phantoms, and not realities. Lewis has a surprising statement of the implications of the point in *A Grief Observed*. It comes early in the book, where Lewis has been wondering if non-believing naturalist explanations might not be right. In other words humans might be material configurations which have thrown up strange properties, so that Lewis's wife Joy was no more than this. Lewis sees that this is to relegate his wife to non-existence in fact, so that if this is what she was, she never really "existed" at all. The statement is astonishing in its stark simplicity, and shows how Christian views of immortality or afterlife, cohere with a deep and powerful ontology of this-worldly entities. He says: "If Helen 'is not,' then she never was. I mistook a cloud of atoms for a person. There aren't, and never were, any people. Death only reveals the vacuity that was always there. What we call the living are simply those who have not yet been unmasked. All equally bankrupt, but some not yet declared."[39]

---

38. Aristotle, *Generation of Animals*, 171.
39. Lewis, *A Grief Observed*, 25.

5

God and the Moral Law in C. S. Lewis

MATTHEW FLANNAGAN

THIS CHAPTER CRITICALLY EXAMINES C. S. Lewis's position on the relationship between God and the moral law. The discussion proceeds in four stages. In section 2, I will briefly summarise Lewis's meta-ethical argument for the existence of God, which occurs in the early chapters of *Mere Christianity*. I will suggest that a natural reading of this argument is that Lewis was contending that the nature of moral obligations is best accounted for by identifying them with the commands of God and hence Lewis was advocating a divine command theory of moral obligation. However, I will note that an examination of Lewis's other writings on the subject show that Lewis explicitly rejected a divine command theory and instead articulated a position on God and the moral law which, *prima facie*, is subject to metaphysical difficulties.

In section 2, I ask why this is the case. Why did Lewis reject a theory that followed naturally from his argument, in favor of a position subject to these difficulties? The answer is that Lewis accepted an ancient objection often thought to be devastating against divine command theories. This objection is known as the Euthyphro dilemma. In several places Lewis appropriated this objection to divine command theories and concluded such theories are unacceptable. The rest of this paper critiques Lewis's appropriation of the Euthyphro dilemma. In section 3 I will argue that Lewis's objections to a divine command theory were unsound. The provisional conclusion in Section IV is that Lewis's position in *Mere Christianity* can be improved by the adoption of a divine command theory.

C. S. LEWIS AND THE META-ETHICAL ARGUMENT FOR GOD'S EXISTENCE

In *Mere Christianity*, C. S. Lewis began his famous discussion of Christianity by offering a moral argument for the existence of God. In these chapters Lewis examined some of the presuppositions of moral argumentation (which Lewis called a quarrel). Lewis stressed three things. First, that moral discourse presupposes the existence of some "standard of behavior"[1] which Lewis called a law. Second, this law is known; protagonists in moral argument "expect the other man to know about [it]."[2] Third, Lewis stressed the objectivity of this law. Lewis argued that this law is "a real law, which none of us have made, but which we find pressing on us."[3] It is not a social convention,[4] nor is it simply an evolved herd instinct.[5] Lewis stressed the objectivity of moral obligations again in "The Poison of Subjectivism," where he defended the existence of an objective "natural law" against contemporary relativism and subjectivism.

The word "law" plays a key role in this argument; laws require lawgivers, so contending an objective moral law exists, suggests that an intelligent person, who exists independently of human beings, is behind it. Critics of moral arguments for God's existence contend such arguments are unsound, as they equivocate on this word "law." Peter Bryne states a law can either be a "deliverance from some person or body of persons" or "a rule with authority."[6] He cites laws of logic as examples of the second sort. These have *rational* authority but are not obviously promulgated by an authority the way we say a statute law is.

I think however, Lewis's point can be made without using the ambiguous term "law." What I think Lewis was getting at is that obligations are, as Robert Adams suggests, *social* requirements. Adams argues that being

1. Lewis, *Mere Christianity*, 3.
2. Ibid.
3. Ibid.
4. Ibid., 10–11.
5. Ibid., 8–10.
6. Bryne, "Moral Arguments."

obligated to do X differs from it being rational to do X, or it being good to do X, in that you *have* to do X. If you fail to do X, it is appropriate for other people to blame you and to censure you for your failure. Such failure makes you guilty: a state which is expiated by gaining forgiveness. Adams argues that all these features, which are unique to obligations, strongly suggest that "being obligated to do something consists in being required (in a certain way under certain situations) by another person or groups of persons not to do it."[7] Obligations are a kind of social relationship where one person makes a demand on another.[8] This feature of obligation, including moral obligation, makes it very different to laws of logic. While we can talk about "laws" of logic, people don't generally refer to these as obligations. We talk of social obligations, or financial obligations, or legal obligations, but not logical ones; this is because obligations are demands on people, made by another.

By referring to moral obligations as a "law" Lewis had in mind the social nature of obligations. This is suggested by the conclusion Lewis drew in the fourth chapter of *Mere Christianity*. Here he argued that theism provides a better explanation and account of the existence of this law than naturalism does. He wrote:

> If there was a controlling influence outside the universe, it would not show itself to us as one of the facts inside the universe-no more than an architect of a house could actually be a wall or staircase or fireplace in that house. The only way we could expect it to show itself would be inside ourselves as an *influence or command trying to get us to behave in a certain way. And that is just what we do find inside ourselves.* . . . All I have got to is a Something which is directing the universe, and which appears in me as a law *urging me to do right and making me feel responsible and uncomfortable when I do wrong.* I think we have to assume it is more like a mind than it is like anything else we know—because after all the only other

---

7. Adams, *Finite and Infinite Goods*, 242.

8. Lewis argues only that the existence of the moral law provides evidence of some mind or person behind the Universe who desires that we do what is right. He does not claim it provides proof of full blown Christian theism. However, Lewis is here perhaps being too modest; the claim that the best account of the nature of moral wrongness is that they are the commands of some supernatural intelligence is defensible only if God is understood to be both virtuous and omniscient—if he is vicious or ignorant then there are possible worlds in which he commands evil actions and hence moral wrongness will not be identical with that being's prohibitions.

> thing we *know is matter and you can hardly imagine a bit of matter giving instructions.*[9]

Lewis here refers to the moral law as an instruction, command or demand made by another person, one that brings with it social pressure, such as blame, and guilt.

In chapter 5, Lewis summarized the previous discussion "I ended my last chapter with the idea that *in the Moral law somebody or something from beyond the natural universe was actually getting to us.*"[10] Lewis stated that the moral law which humans perceive in their conscience *simply is a set of commands* or instructions issued to human beings by God. A natural way to read these passages is to see Lewis as having proposed a divine command theory of ethics. According to a divine command theory moral obligations are constituted by (or identified with) God's commands. Taken this way, Lewis was arguing that theism is more plausible than naturalism because a theist can provide a more adequate account of the nature of the moral obligation—what Lewis calls the moral law—by identifying this law with the commands of God.[11] Naturalism does not allow for the existence of a transcendent person who could make demands of the type which are presupposed in moral discourse.

This seems the most straightforward way of reading Lewis's argument. If it is correct, Lewis was offering a simplified version of "The Meta-Ethical Argument" advocated by Robert Adams and popularized by William Lane Craig. In fact there are striking similarities between Lewis's argument and the argument which Adams proposed. Adams summarized the argument this way

> We believe quite firmly that certain things are morally right and others are morally wrong (for example, that it is wrong to torture another person to death just for fun). Questions may be raised about the nature of that which is believed in these beliefs: what does the rightness or wrongness of an act consist in? I believe that the most adequate answer is provided by a theory that entails the existence of God—specifically, by the theory that moral rightness and wrongness consist in agreement and disagreement, respectively, with the will or commands of a loving God. One of the

---

9. Lewis, *Mere Christianity*, 18–20 (emphasis added).

10. Ibid., 22 (emphasis added).

11. It's worth noting here that if one grants this point, it follows only that all else being equal the existence of right and wrong makes theism more probable than naturalism.

most generally accepted reasons for believing in the existence of anything is that its existence is implied by the theory that seems to account most adequately for some subject matter. I take it, therefore, that my metaethical views provide me with a reason of some weight for believing in the existence of God.[12]

Crucial to this argument is the claim that the most adequate answer to the question of what "rightness and wrongness consist in" is the "theory that moral rightness and wrongness consist in agreement and disagreement, respectively, with the will or commands of a loving God."

Interestingly, Adams defended this premise in a manner similar to Lewis. Like Lewis, Adams described certain features of moral obligation which an analysis of moral discourse discloses. Adams contended "wrongness is the property which best accounts for the role assigned it by the concept." He argued the relevant property should be; (a) a property of actions, (b) objective, (c) able to account for the wrongness of the major portions of actions we consider to be wrong, (d) play a causal role in our coming to know what is wrong, and (e) be seen as a supremely weighty reason against doing the action.[13] The stress on the objectivity of moral obligations, and that they are known, is an obvious parallel with Lewis. Moreover, as Adams argued, the role of guilt, censure, punishment, and forgiveness, as well as social inculcation, suggest obligations are social requirements.[14] Hence Adams, like Lewis, argued that our moral discourse presupposes something like a "law" where a person demands us to do certain things, a demand backed with associated social pressure of guilt, censure and so forth, and this law is objective and known. But Adams added that the demand attaches to those actions which we recognize as wrong, and provides a supremely weighty reason for doing those actions.

Similarly, Adams, like Lewis, argued that divine commands best explain these features of moral obligation by comparing two conditionals: Adams argued that if theism is true a divine command theory is a more plausible account of the nature of right and wrong than any other theory is in the absence of theistic assumptions. If one assumes God exists one has a defensible account of the nature of wrongness which fits (a)-(e), much better than any account which is not based on naturalistic or atheistic assumptions. If God exists one can make sense of the fact that moral obligations

12. Adams, "Moral Arguments for Theistic Belief," 145.
13. Adams, "Divine Command," 74–76.
14. See n7.

are social requirements, are objective, known, attach to those actions we recognise as wrong, and have overriding rational authority, in a way that one cannot if one does not assume God exists.[15]

So a natural way of reading Lewis here is to see him as having anticipated Adams's meta-ethical argument for theism and defending a divine command theory of the nature of moral obligations. Such a reading, however, is at odds with what Lewis said on the matter elsewhere. In several other places Lewis refused to identify our moral obligations with God's commands. In *The Problem of Pain* for example, Lewis wrote,

> It is sometimes asked whether God commands things because they are right, or whether they are right because God commands them. With Hooker, and against Dr Johnson I affirm the first alternative. ... God's will is determined by his wisdom which always perceives, and his goodness which always embraces, the intrinsically good. ... The content of our obedience-the thing we are commanded to do-will always be something intrinsically good, something we ought to do even if (by impossible supposition) God had not commanded it.[16]

Here Lewis stated that the moral law exists independently of God. Being all-knowing God accurately discerns its content, and being all-good embraces the standards the law lays down, and as a result commands us to obey it. However, the law exists independently of God's commands and would exist and bind us even if God did not command it.

This picture of the relationship between God and the moral law however seems *prima facie* problematic for at least three reasons.

First, it appears to clash with God's aseity, the idea that everything distinct from God is dependent upon him. On the face of it Lewis postulated the existence of a law which is independent of and prior to God's willing or commanding.[17]

Second, this position is, *prima facie*, inconsistent with the argument of *Mere Christianity*. In *Mere Christianity* Lewis suggested that the nature and

---

15. Adams, "Prospects for a Meta-ethical argument for Theism," 316. William Lane Craig has similarly defended a divine command theory by defending two conditionals. (1) If God exists we have a solid foundation for moral duties, and (2) if God does not exist we do not have a solid foundation of moral duties. See Craig "This Most Gruesome of Guests," 169.

16. Lewis, *The Problem of Pain*, 409.

17. Alvin Plantinga makes this point about the existence of abstract objects in general in "Does God Have a Nature?," in *The Analytic Theist*, 226–56.

existence of the moral law is better explained by the existence of a divine mind than it is on naturalism. The position expressed in *The Problem of Pain* appears to make the moral law ontologically independent of the divine mind so the law would exist and remain binding even if God did not exist. All the features of the moral law such as its objectivity, and rational authority would need to be accounted for independently of God.

Third, Lewis's position appears to clash with the idea that God is a being who has supreme and total allegiance over us. Note that Lewis suggested that we are required to obey God only if he commands us to obey a law which exists and has authority independently of him. Hence it appears that there exists something other than God that has authority over us, and would bind us even if God did not exist or God commanded otherwise. God's authority is subordinate to the moral law.

In "The Poison of Subjectivism" Lewis realized this problem. "[T]he other objection is much more formidable. If we grant that our practical reason is really reason and that its fundamental imperatives are as absolute and categorical as they claim to be, then unconditional allegiance to them is the duty of man. So is absolute allegiance to God."

Lewis's solution was to argue:

> When we attempt to think of a person and a law, we are compelled to think of this person either as obeying the law or as making it. And when we think of Him as making it we are compelled to think of Him either as making it in conformity to some yet more ultimate pattern of goodness (in which case that pattern, and not He, would be supreme) or else as making it arbitrarily. . . . But it is probably just here that our categories betray us. It would be idle, with our merely mortal resources, to attempt a positive correction of our categories. . . . But it might be permissible to lay down two negations: that God neither *obeys* nor *creates* the moral law. The good is uncreated; it could never have been otherwise; it has in it no shadow of contingency; it lies, as Plato said, on the other side of existence. [But since only God admits of no contingency, we must say that] God is not merely good, but goodness; goodness is not merely divine, but God.[18]

Here Lewis suggested that God *is* the moral law. He was speaking literally here. We sometimes talk about a person such as a sheriff or police officer being "the law" but this loose language is used to convey the idea that such people enforce the law in some way. Lewis however made a claim

18. Lewis, "The Poison of Subjectivism," 107–8.

of strict identity. God *is* the moral law. This claim however is ontologically quite weird. A law and a person seem to be two quite different entities. A law can be an expression of a person's will or commands laid down *by* a person, but the idea that a law in and of itself could *be* a person, that properties such as rightness and wrongness being obligated or prohibited are in fact a conscious, living, rational person, certainly seems on the face of it to involve a category mistake.

Lewis seemed to be aware of this problem. He stated "[w]hen we attempt to think of a person and a law, we are compelled to think of this person either as obeying the law or as making it." He suggested as a solution "that our categories betray us." He admitted that what he proposed sounds metaphysically absurd but this is because our ontological intuitions or and categories are mistaken. Lewis in fact referred to his position as "fine spun speculations." Regardless of what one thinks about the cogency of this response one can see immediately that the explanation of the moral law proposed by Adams is a *prima facie* better explanation. The idea that the moral law is God's law is fairly simple and straightforward. It postulates that a law is a law, that a law expresses a person's commands and will, and does not entail that the law is *itself* a person. No violence to our ontological categories is necessary. We do not need to reject plausible metaphysical assumptions. Nor does a divine command theory raise any questions about God's aseity or make him subject to some set of mysterious abstract principles that exist independently of him. This raises the question, why didn't Lewis simply adopt a divine command theory?

C. S. LEWIS AND THE EUTHYPHRO OBJECTION

The answer is that Lewis believed that "nothing short of [his position on God and the moral law] can save us." It is clear from his writings that Lewis believed a divine command theory was philosophically untenable and subject to a crippling objection. He cited the objection he has in mind several times.

In "The Poison of Subjectivism," Lewis wrote,

> [H]ow is the relation between God and the moral law to be represented? To say that the moral law is God's law is no final solution. Are these things right because God commands them or does God command them because they are right? If the first, if good is to be *defined* as what God commands, then the goodness

of God Himself is emptied of meaning and the commands of an omnipotent fiend would have the same claim on us as those of the "righteous Lord." If the second, then we seem to be admitting a cosmic diarchy, or even making God Himself the mere executor of a law somehow external and antecedent to His own being. Both views are intolerable. . . .

When we attempt to think of a person and a law, we are compelled to think of this person either as obeying the law or as making it. And when we think of Him as making it we are compelled to think of Him either as making it in conformity to some yet more ultimate pattern of goodness (in which case that pattern, and not He, would be supreme) or else as making it arbitrarily. [19]

In *Reflections on the Psalms* Lewis raised the same line of argument.

There were in the eighteenth century terrible theologians who held that "God did not command certain things because they are right, but certain things are right because God commanded them." To make the position perfectly clear, one of them even said that though God has, as it happens, commanded us to love Him and one another, He might equally well have commanded us to hate Him and one another, and hatred would then have been right. It was apparently a mere toss-up which He decided on. Such a view in effect makes God a mere arbitrary tyrant. It would be better and less irreligious to believe in no God and to have no ethics than to have such an ethics and such a theology as this.[20]

It's worth summarizing the argument Lewis proposed in these passages. It proceeded in two stages.

First, Lewis suggested that a person who believes in both a God who commands right conduct, and also an objective moral law faces a dilemma; either he or she holds that something is right because God commands it, or he or she maintains that God commands it because it right. This is evident from several things he said. He stated that to hold that "the moral law is God's law is no final solution." Instead one faces the question "Are these things right because God commands them or does God command them because they are right?" He stated that "we are compelled" to think of God "either as obeying the law or as making it."

Second, Lewis in all these citations rejected the first horn of this dilemma option. Two reasons are provided.

19. Ibid.
20. Lewis, *Reflections on the Psalms*, 54.

First, Lewis suggested that the first horn: the contention that things are right because God commands them, makes God's commands arbitrary. Lewis contended that eighteenth-century theologians which embraced the first horn held that although "God has, as it happens, commanded us to love Him and one another, He might equally well have commanded us to hate Him" and "It was apparently a mere toss-up which He decided." This makes "God a mere arbitrary tyrant." I will refer to this argument as "the arbitrariness objection."

Second, the first horn makes the attribution of goodness to God redundant. If "good is to be *defined* as what God commands, then the goodness of God Himself is emptied of meaning." I will call this the "emptiness objection."

This line of argument was not unique to Lewis nor did it originate with him. He was citing a line of argument which originates in Plato's famous dialogue *The Euthyphro*. The current version, used against monotheistic religions, such as Christianity, Islam and Judaism, is an adaptation of Plato's argument.[21] The argument is something of a cliché in contemporary discussions of God and morality and is widely believed to provide a decisive rebuttal of a divine command theory. Lewis then was in good company in rejecting a divine command theory on the basis of this argument. However, I will argue that Lewis was mistaken to accept this objection. I will examine each step of the argument in turn.

WHY LEWIS SHOULD HAVE REJECTED THE EUTHYPHRO DILEMMA

1. Does the theist who believes in a moral law face the Euthyphro dilemma?

Lewis believed we are "compelled" to face the question "Are these things right because God commands them or does God command them because they are right?" This assumed that the relationship between moral obligations and God's commands is an asymmetrical, dependence relationship that leaves two mutually-exclusive possibilities; either being right is

---

21. Plato's original argument applied to polytheistic religions. Because Socrates's interlocutor took the Homeric stories literally, he faced the problem that there were many deities who all disagreed with each other, often for petty reasons.

ontologically prior to God's commanding, or God's commanding is ontologically prior to what is right.

However there seems no reason for making this assumption. Robert Adams has defended the view that "ethical wrongness is (i.e., is identical with) the property of being contrary to a loving God."[22] This does not expound an asymmetrical relationship but a relationship of identity. Identity relations are symmetrical. So the Euthyphro dilemma simply does not apply to a relationship of identity. To ask which of two identical things was ontologically prior to the other is to ask whether something was prior to itself. An absurd question.

Lewis seemed aware of this response and dismissed it stating "To say that the moral law is God's law is no final solution. Are these things right because God commands them or does God command them because they are right?" However, to simply state that one option is "no solution" is not a reason for thinking it is not a solution. In the absence of some argument why this option is unviable, Lewis's response was mere assertion.

2. The arbitrariness objection

Suppose however we grant that theists are subject to the Euthyphro dilemma. Why does adopting the first horn, the position that actions are right *because* God commands them entail God's commands are arbitrary? *Prima facie* this appears to be a non-sequitur; the fact that God does not prohibit things because they are wrong does not entail that He has *no reason* at all for prohibiting them.

Lewis's reasons for this conclusion are not entirely clear. In the quote from "The Poison of Subjectivism" he simply stated that a divine command theory makes God's commands arbitrary. However in the quote from *Reflections on the Psalms* he offers three reasons, each of which is clearly fallacious.

First, Lewis noted that some "eighteenth century terrible theologians" held this view. However calling people "terrible" is not an argument.

Second, Lewis claimed that one of these theologians, whom he identifies in *The Problem of Pain* as William Paley,[23] held that "though God has, as it happens, commanded us to love Him and one another, He might equally well have commanded us to hate Him." But, even if this is an accurate

---

22. Adams, "Divine Command Meta-Ethics Modified Again," 76.
23. Lewis, *The Problem of Pain*, 409.

rendition of Paley's position (and I suspect it is not) the fact that one theologian held this view does not mean that all divine command theorists do, nor does it entail a divine command theorist must hold this view.

Third, Lewis took Paley's position to entail "It was apparently a mere toss-up which He decided on." But this does not follow. The fact that one could have done something different to what one in fact did does not entail that your decision was "a mere toss-up."

So, Lewis's articulation of the arbitrariness objection has a lot to be desired. Despite this I think there is a sensible line of objection which Lewis alludes to. Mark Murphy notes that "an extraordinarily popular charge" against a divine command theory is "that it entails, objectionably, that morality is arbitrary." He distinguishes two versions of this objection. "One claim is that theological voluntarism implies that God's commands/intentions, on which moral statuses depend, must be arbitrary," and the second is "that theological voluntarism implies that the content of morality is itself arbitrary."[24]

I suspect Lewis has conflated these two objections. When Lewis contended, "It was apparently a mere toss-up which [God] decided on" he alluded to the first of these objections, and when he claimed that although "God has, as it happens, commanded us to love Him and one another, He might equally well have commanded us to hate Him" he alluded to the second.

Do divine commands have an arbitrary basis?

Wes Moriston has recently summed up the first of these objections

> Either God has good reasons for his commands or he does not. If he does, then those reasons (and not God's commands) are the ultimate ground of moral obligation. If he does not have good reasons, then his commands are completely arbitrary and may be disregarded. Either way, the divine command theory is false.[25]

This objection commits the fallacy of equivocation. Consider the following argument.

---

24. Murphy, *Theological Voluntarism*.
25. Wes Morriston, "God and the Ontological Foundation of Morality."

[1] Either God has good reasons for his commands or he does not.

[2] If he does have good reasons for his commands then those reasons (and not God's commands) are the ultimate ground of moral obligation.

[3] If he does not have good reasons for his commands then his commands are completely arbitrary and may be disregarded.

Therefore:

[4] Either God's commands are not the ultimate grounds of moral obligation or they may be disregarded.

The problem is that the word "reasons" is ambiguous. William Wainwright has pointed out that the word "reason" can be used in two different senses.[26] The first is a *constitutive* sense. This sense occurs when one explains one thing by identifying it with another. Consider the case where a person affirms that the *reason* water has certain properties is *because* it is H2O. When the word "reason" is used in this sense, the use of the word "reason" denotes a relationship of identity; one is saying that water is identical with H2O.

The second sense is a *motivational* reason. This sense occurs when one identifies factors that motivate a particular action. For example, the reason I feed my daughter is because I love her and feeding her is an important part ensuring her flourishing. This sense is more psychological and epistemic and does not refer to a relationship of identity.

It is important to note that these two senses are not the same as the following illustration demonstrates. My son Noah fills a glass with water. If we ask what the constitutive reason was for his action, the answer would be that he filled the glass with water because he filled the glass with H2O. If we ask what the motivational reason was for his action, the answer would be that he wanted a drink. Yet his wanting a drink does not constitute water; likewise, water being H2O is not the motivational reason for him filling the glass.

Turning back to the premise: [1] "Either God has good reasons for his commands or he does not." When the objector makes this claim he could be talking about whether God has motivating reasons for his commands or he could be asking if there are constitutive reasons for his commands.

If the objector is referring to a motivating reason then the third premise of the argument is correct; if God has no *motivating* reasons for

---

26. Wainwright, *Religion and Morality*, 91.

commanding as he does then his commands are arbitrary. To avoid the conclusion that God's commands are arbitrary one would have to concede that God has motivating reasons for issuing them.

The problem is that on this sense of "reason," the second premise of the argument is false. If God does have motivating reasons then it does not follow that those reasons (and not God's commands) are the ultimate *ground* of moral obligation. This is because when people claim that God is the ultimate ground of moral obligation, they typically mean that moral obligations are *identified* with God's commands. In other words, they claim that God's commands are the *constitutive* reason for our moral obligations. But the fact that one has a *motivating* reason for an action does not mean that these reasons *constitute* the action. I noted this in the example I gave above; the fact that Noah has a *motivating* reason to pour water into a glass does not mean that these motivations *constitute* him pouring water into the glass. What constitutes water are H2o molecules, *not* Noah's motivations.

This brings us to the second option. Perhaps in premise [1] the objector is not referring to a motivating reason, rather he is referring to some kind of constitutive reason. This might enable the objector to sensibly claim that the second premise is true. If something other than and prior to God's commands is identical with moral obligations then God's commands will not be the ultimate ground of moral obligation. The problem is that if this is what is meant by the word "reason" then the third premise is false. Even if God does not have *constitutive* reasons for his commands, he could still have *motivating* reasons for issuing them. If God has motivational reasons for issuing the commands he does, such as concern for the welfare of others, then God's commands are not arbitrary. So this argument commits the fallacy of equivocation.

Does a divine command theory mean the content of morality is arbitrary?

Perhaps at the heart of Lewis's argument however was the concern that a divine command theory makes the content of morality arbitrary. This appears to be the issue in Lewis's complaint that Paley's divine command theory, that "though God has, as it happens, commanded us to love Him and one another, He might equally well have commanded us to hate Him."

GOD AND THE MORAL LAW IN C. S. LEWIS

Here Lewis alluded to an extremely common objection. This objection was pressed forcefully by Michael Tooley, in a debate he had with William Lane Craig at the University of Colorado. Tooley stated,

> There is a theory which has the consequence that there cannot be objective moral laws unless God exists—that's the so-called "divine command theory of morality." What it says is that an action is wrong because and only because God forbids it. And an action is obligatory because and only because God demands it. If that theory were right, then there would be an argument in support of the claim that Dr. Craig has advanced. But that theory is quite a hopeless theory because of its implications. One of its implications, for example, is that if God had commanded mankind to torture one another as much as possible, then it would follow that that action was obligatory. Perhaps Dr. Craig would be happy with that consequence. But many people, including many religious thinkers, are very unhappy with that consequence, and so have rejected the divine command theory of morality. [27]

Tooley's concerns have been echoed by others. For example, Robert K. Garcia and Nathan L. King have objected: "DCT [divine command theory] implies that it is possible for any kind of action, such as rape, to not be wrong. But it seems intuitively impossible for rape not to be wrong. So, DCT is at odds with our commonsense intuitions about rape."[28]

A similar line of argument has been made by David Brink.

> We might also notice a counter intuitive implication of voluntarism. Voluntarism implies that all moral truths are contingent on what God happens to approve.... Thus, for example, had God had not condemned genocide and rape, these things would not have been wrong, or, if God were to approve these things they would become morally acceptable. But these are awkward commitments, inasmuch as this sort of conduct seems necessarily wrong. [29]

Brink here used the example of genocide[30] and rape; however, I suggest that he would say the same thing about Tooley's example of a com-

27. Tooley, "Opening Statement."
28. Garcia and King, introduction to *Is Goodness without God Good Enough?*, 11.
29. Brink, "The Autonomy of Ethics," 152.
30. Some might object here that the Bible teaches that God did command genocide. The book of Deuteronomy records that God then commanded Israel to "destroy totally" the people occupying these regions (the Canaanites); the Israelites were to "not leave alive anything that breathes" (20:16). The book of Joshua records the carrying out of this

mand to "torture one another as much as possible" hence, for clarity I will stick with Tooley's example. Wes Moriston has summarised this objection as follows: Let X = the action of torturing one another as much as possible.

[1] The divine command theory entails that whatever God commands is morally obligatory.

[2] God could command X.

[3] So if the divine command theory is true, X could be morally obligatory,

[4] but X could not be morally obligatory;

[5] therefore, the divine command theory is false.[31]

This objection assumes [2] is true; that it is possible that God could command atrocious things like torturing people for fun. However, this seems dubious. Tooley has defined God as an "omnipotent, omniscient, and *morally perfect* [emphasis added]."[32] Similarly, in his debate with Craig he stated,

> I want to begin by briefly indicating how I'm going to understand the term "God" in this next discussion. My view is that the question one should ask is, "What characteristics should an object possess in order to be an appropriate object of religious attitudes?"
>
> I think that the answer to that is that a being, to be characterizable as God in that sense, should be a personal being, *should be a being that is morally perfect*, a being that is omnipotent, and a being that is omniscient [emphasis added].[33]

So, as Tooley defines his terms, the claim that there is a possible world where God commands people to "torture one another as much as possible"

---

command. In the sixth chapter it states: "they devoted the city to the Lord and destroyed with the sword every living thing in it—men and women, young and old, cattle, sheep and donkeys" (v. 21). Several chapters later, we read that Joshua "left no survivors. He totally destroyed all who breathed, just as the Lord, the God of Israel, had commanded" (10:40; 11:14). The text mentions city after city where Joshua, at God's command, puts every inhabitant "to the sword," "totally destroyed the inhabitants" and "left no survivors" (10:28, 30, 33, 37, 39, 40; 11:8). For a response to this kind of argument see my articles "Did God Command Canaanite Genocide?" and also "Some Reflections on the Ethics of Yahweh Wars." In both these papers I argue that a careful reading of the relevant texts in their canonical context, suggests they are highly hyperbolized hagiographic accounts and not intended to be taken as literally true.

31. Moriston, "What if God Commanded Something Terrible?," 251.

32. Tooley, "Does God Exist?," 72.

33. Tooley and Craig, *A Classic Debate on the Existence of God*.

is true only if there is a possible world where a morally perfect omniscient person would command this action.

This is unlikely. The very reason Tooley cited the example, of "torturing others as much as possible," is because he views it as a paradigm of an action that no morally good person could ever knowingly entertain. Similarly, Brink mentioned actions like rape and genocide because he thinks it is impossible that any rational and virtuous person could be endorse such actions. But, if this is the case, then a morally perfect being would never command such actions. The argument by Tooley, Garcia, King and Brink, is unsound, hence Lewis's worries were unfounded.

The emptiness objection

This response brings us to the second objection Lewis raised to the first horn of the Euthyphro dilemma.

> [H]ow is the relation between God and the moral law to be represented? To say that the moral law is God's law is no final solution. Are these things right because God commands them or does God command them because they are right? If the first, if good is to be *defined* as what God commands, then the goodness of God Himself is emptied of meaning and the commands of an omnipotent fiend would have the same claim on us as those of the "righteous Lord" [emphasis added]. [34]

There are clear problems with this argument as Lewis has formulated it. Lewis began by suggesting the options are either that actions are "right because God commands them" or that God commands them "because they are right." However, when he characterized the "first" option, he described it, not as the claim that actions are "right because God commands them." But rather as the claim that "good is to be *defined* as what God commands." These two positions however are not the same. They differ in at least two respects.

First, as noted previously, the claim that actions are right *because* God commands them suggests that God's commands makes or brings it about that certain actions are right. This presupposes that the relationship between moral obligations and God commands is some kind of asymmetrical dependence relationship where one entity in the relationship is temporally

---

34. Lewis, "The Poison of Subjectivism," 106.

or ontologically prior to the other. Definitions on the other hand are not typically asymmetric dependence relationships at all. Definitions provide an analysis of what various terms mean, or how various concepts are to be understood, and it does this by showing how other more basic concepts relate to them.

In fact, if "good is to be *defined* as what God commands" it is difficult to see why the Euthyphro dilemma applies at all. Consider the following example. A person tells you that a bachelor is an unmarried man because the term "bachelor" is defined as "an unmarried man." It would not make sense to respond to this by asking, "is he a bachelor because he is unmarried or is he unmarried because he is a bachelor?" A person's unmarried-ness is not prior to or the cause of his bachelorhood nor is his bachelorhood the cause of his being unmarried. Saying he is unmarried is just a different way of referring to his bachelorhood. The relationship between a bachelor and an unmarried man is not a relationship of ontological dependence; the relationship is one of meaning.

Second, the claim that actions are "right because God commands them" makes reference to what makes things *right*, not to what is good in general. The word "right" limits this claim to the deontological properties of actions, "whether it has such properties as being morally permitted, being morally forbidden or prohibited, and being morally obligatory or required."[35] The claim however that *good* is defined as what God commands is not limited to deontological properties this way. The distinction between what makes an action right and what is good is important. Stephen Evans has noted, "it does not appear that the concept of obligation is identical to the concept of that which it is 'good to do.' Many acts are good in this sense without being obligatory."[36] He provided an example, "It might be good, or even saintly, for me to give a kidney to benefit a stranger, but it is not an act I am obliged to do."[37]

So an initial problem with Lewis's argument is that he did not actually rebut the claim that actions are right because God commands them. Instead he argued against a different proposition altogether.

It is also worth noting that the claim Lewis did refute is a strawman. Because few, if any, divine command theorists, whether historical or contemporary, have held that "good is to be defined as God commands."

---

35. Quinn, "An Argument for Divine Command Theory," 291.
36. Evans, *Kierkegaard's Ethic of Love*, 16.
37. Ibid.

Typically divine command theories are limited to deontological properties. For example, Philip Quinn limited his theory to deontological properties and was not offering a divine command theory of broader axiological properties such as goodness.[38] In this he was followed by Adams,[39] William Alston,[40] Craig,[41] Edward Wierenga,[42] John Hare,[43] Alvin Plantinga,[44] and even to some extent Thomas Carson.[45] Neither is this unique to contemporary divine command theories. Locke,[46] Puffendorf, Paley, and Berkley[47] similarly limited their theories to deontological properties, and not to broader axiological properties such as goodness.

Not only are divine command theories limited to deontological properties, but they do not typically offer an analysis of the meaning of moral terms. As noted previously, Robert Adams defended the contention that "ethical wrongness *is [identical with]* the property of being contrary to the commands of a loving God [emphasis added]."[48] Adams drew on developments in contemporary philosophy of language[49] which distinguish between a term being conceptually analyzed in terms of another term, and the referent of both terms being identical. A famous example of this distinction is the relationship between water and H2o. Water is H2o. This is a claim of identity. The liquid on earth that we call water is hydrogen hydroxide. However, the claim that water is H2o is not an analytic truth that is true in virtue of the meaning of the words. It is a claim discovered by empirical investigation. A competent language user could refer to water and understand the

---

38. Quinn "An Argument for Divine Command Theory," 291.

39. Adams, "Divine Command Meta-Ethics Modified Again," 74–76, and *Finite and Infinite Goods*.

40. Alston, "Some Suggestions for Divine Command Theorists," 303–4.

41. Craig, *Philosophical Foundations*, 529–32.

42. Weirenga, *The Nature of God*, 215–27. See also "Utilitarianism and the Divine Command Theory," and "A Defensible Divine Command Theory."

43. Hare, *God's Call*, and *God and Morality*.

44. Plantinga, "Naturalism, Theism, Obligation and Supervenience."

45. Carson, *Value and the Good Life*.

46. For a defence of the claim that Locke was a divine command theorist, see Oakley and Urdang, "Locke, Natural Law and God."

47. Paley, "Principles"; Broad, "Berkeley's Theory of Morals"; Darwall, "Berkeley's Moral and Political Philosophy."

48. Adams, "Divine Command Meta-Ethics Modified Again," 76.

49. See for example Putnam, "The Meaning of Meaning"; Donnellan, "Reference and Definite Descriptions"; Kripke, "Naming and Necessity."

meaning of this term without needing to know about the atomic structure H20. By distinguishing between identity and meaning, Adams explicitly denied he is proposing the position Lewis criticised. Evans, Alston,[50] and Craig[51] all follow Adams's lead on this.

Even those who haven't followed Adams do not propose an analysis of moral terms. Quinn argued that God's commands cause or bring about deontological properties but specifically denies that the relationship between God's commands and deontological properties is one of meaning.[52] Edward Weirenga[53] and John Hare[54] have defended similar positions. The same is true historically. In the past divine command theorists usually proposed theories about what makes actions right and wrong and not theories about the meaning of moral terms.[55]

So Lewis criticises a straw man. One might say I am being unfair to Lewis here. The contemporary revival of divine command theories, seen in the writings of people like Quinn, Adams, Hare and so on, occurred well after Lewis wrote. This charge has some justification if we take it as an attack on Lewis himself, though the reference to historical divine command theories in my above summary goes some way to blunting this charge.[56] However, even if it is unfair to criticise Lewis in this way, if we are to assess Lewis's ideas in terms of their contemporary applicability his arguments do miss their mark. In order for a contemporary appropriation of Lewis's argument to be something other than a straw man, it needs to be reformulated to deal with theories like the ones actually proposed by defenders of divine command meta-ethics.

---

50. Alston "Some Suggestions," 303–4

51. Craig, "This Most Gruesome of Guests," 186.

52. Quinn, "An Argument for Divine Command Theory," 293.

53. Weirenga, *The Nature of God*, 215–27. See also "Utilitarianism and the Divine Command Theory," and "A Defensible Divine Command Theory."

54. Hare, *God's Call*, 49.

55. Idziak, "In Search of Good Positive Reasons," 60.

56. Consider for example William Paley, whom Lewis cites as an example of a divine command theorist. Paley distinguished between what was good and what was right. Paley is often portrayed as a utilitarian due to the fact that he considered happiness to be good and argued a good person would promote the general happiness of humankind. He contended however, that right and wrong were based on divine commands. God, being good, sought the happiness of human beings as his goal and issues commands to humans which, if followed by all people, would promote happiness.

Divine Duties and Divine Perfection

Such a reformulation was recently suggested by Peter Van Inwagen. According to a divine command theory the wrongness of an action consists in its being forbidden by God, however, given that God does not issue commands to himself it follows that God has no duties. Some divine command theorists have insisted on this fact. Craig has argued that "[duties] are not independent of God nor, plausibly, is God bound by moral duties, since He does not issue commands to Himself." Similarly, Alston has argued, "we can hardly suppose that God is obliged to love his creatures because he commands himself to do so!" Wainwright has even suggested that "the notion of commanding oneself to do something . . . is incoherent."[57]

In *The Problem of Evil*, Peter Van Inwagen has argued that if God has no duties then "presumably, there is no such property or attribute as 'moral perfection.'" He argued "If there is no such attribute as moral perfection, the *aliquid quo nihil maius cogitari possit*[58] will not be morally perfect—and not because it will be morally imperfect, but because there will not be any such thing for it to be."[59]

Why does Van Inwagen think the absence of divine duties entails this? Earlier in the same book he defined moral perfection as follows:

> God has no moral defect whatever. It follows that he is in no way a subject of possible moral criticism. If someone says something of the form, "God did x and it was wrong of God to do x," that person must be mistaken: either God did not in fact do x or it was not wrong of God to do x.[60]

I think Van Inwagen means to argue as follows: a person can be morally perfect, in the sense he defines these terms, only if there is an objective moral standard that applies to that person and that person perfectly conforms to this standard. This is presumably what Van Inwagen meant by, "God has no moral defect whatever." God never goes against the standard of right and wrong that applies to him; God has duties and acts in accord with them. Similarly, when he affirmed "If someone says something of the

---

57. Wainwright, *Religion and Morality*, 116.

58. *Aliquid quo nihil maius cogtari possit* is Latin for "something greater than which nothing can be conceived" referring to Anselm's famous definition of God in the *Proslogion*.

59. Van Inwagen, *The Problem of Evil*, 161.

60. Ibid., 26–27.

form, "God did x and it was wrong of God to do x," that person must be mistaken: either God did not in fact do x or it was not wrong of God to do x," he was suggesting that God has duties and never, in any possible world, acts contrary to them. If moral perfection is understood in this deontological fashion, it follows that if God has no duties he cannot be morally perfect. Of course he cannot be morally imperfect either; to be morally imperfect there would have to be a moral standard that applies to God that God acts contrary to. On Van Inwagen's deontological conception of moral perfection, the property of moral perfection simply does not apply to God.

Van Inwagen is correct that, according to the deontological conception of moral perfection he sketches, the denial of divine duties entails that God is not morally perfect. However, divine command theorists have contended that this really does not amount to much of a criticism because there seems no reason as to why God's moral perfection has to be spelled out deontologically. Mark Murphy notes,

> Granting to some extent the force of the objection, we can say, on this view, that God's moral goodness cannot consist in God's adhering to what is morally obligatory. But there are other ways to assess God morally other than in terms of the morally obligatory. Adams, for example, holds that God should be understood as benevolent and as just, and indeed concedes that his theological voluntarist account of obligation as the divinely commanded is implausible unless God is thus understood.[61] The ascription to God of these moral virtues is entirely consistent with his theological voluntarism, for his theological voluntarism is not meant to provide any account of the moral virtues. One can hold that God's moral goodness involves supereminent possession of the virtues, at least insofar as those virtues do not presuppose weakness and vulnerability. God is good because God is supremely just, loyal, faithful, benevolent, and so forth. It seems that ascribing to God supereminent possession of these virtues would be enough to account for God's supreme moral goodness: it is, after all, in such terms that God is praised in the Psalms.[62]

If God does not have duties, it does not follow that he does not or cannot have certain character traits such as being loving, truthful, benevolent, compassionate, long-suffering, just, that he cannot possess hatred of

---

61. Adams, *Finite and Infinite Goods*, 253–55.
62. Murphy, "Theological Voluntarism."

actions that are, in fact, unjust and various other attributes that are traditionally attributed to God.[63] Van Inwagen is aware of this point.

> But no doubt anyone who felt compelled to remove "moral perfection" from the list of properties a "something" must have if it is to be something than which a greater cannot be conceived (having been convinced by some argument or other that there was no objective moral standard) would want to "replace" it with some attribute whose existence did not presuppose an objective moral standard: "benevolent in the highest possible degree," perhaps, or "exhibiting perfect love toward all creatures."[64]

If God is not "morally perfect" in the deontological sense that Van Inwagen defines this term, this does not preclude attributing goodness in some non-deontological sense to God in a meaningful way in terms of virtues and character traits, hence, in the absence of any argument as to why God's goodness must be construed in a deontological sense, it is hard to see any cogent objection here.

CONCLUSIONS

It is time to bring the threads of this discussion together. In section 1, I noted that C. S. Lewis's argument in *Mere Christianity*, read most naturally, argued for the existence of God on the basis that the nature of moral obligations is best accounted for in terms of divine commands. Moral obligations and the features of guilt, blame, censure, that are conceptually tied with their breach appear to be demands made upon us by another person, in some kind of social relationship, who requires us to act. An analysis of moral discourse suggests these obligations are objective and, something participants in moral discussion expect each other to know about. If God exists, one can plausibly account for the nature of moral obligations by identifying them with Gods commands. If naturalism is true, on the other hand it is hard to account for the existence and nature of something which appears to be both a requirement made by a person and objective and knowable. Elsewhere however, Lewis contradicted this claim. Instead he adopted a position on the moral law which is *prima facie* problematic and considerably less plausible than a divine command theory. The reason Lewis did

---

63. This point has been made repeatedly in the literature, see for example Weirenga *The Nature of God*, 221–22.

64. Van Inwagen, *The Problem of Evil*, 161.

this is because he believed the Euthyphro dilemma constitutes a successful refutation of a divine command theory.

In section 2, I examined Lewis's appropriation of the Euthyphro dilemma and suggested it could be analysed in terms of what I called the arbitrariness objection and the emptiness objection. In section 3, I argued that Lewis's appropriation of both the arbitrariness and emptiness objections fail. I also suggested contemporary developments or versions of Lewis's objections fare no better.

These conclusions suggest that it was a mistake for Lewis to reject a divine command theory. The alternative Lewis suggests has some *prima facie* problems, which a divine command theory lacks, and the reason Lewis rejects a divine command theory are unsound. Moreover, a divine command theory fits his observations in *Mere Christianity*, and the work of contemporary divine command theorists suggests a rigorous way Lewis's metaethical argument can be developed. Lewis's argument in *Mere Christianity* therefore can be improved if one adopts a divine command theory.

6

C. S. Lewis, Animals, and Nature Red in Tooth and Claw

NICOLA HOGGARD CREEGAN

IN THE REMARKABLE BOOK *Life of Pi* by 2002 Booker Prize Winner Yann Martel, we hear the story of a young boy, a zoo keeper's son from India, who is marooned for 277 days on a 26-foot life boat with a live Bengali tiger, a hyena, a zebra, and an orangutan.[1] The hyena, the zebra and the orangutan eat one another or are eaten by the tiger. Only the boy Pi is left, along with the tiger. Before he leaves on this ill-fated journey we find out that he is a very religious child, so religious that he believes in Christianity, Hinduism, and Islam—the more ways of worshipping God the better.

Back to his long journey on the sea, a journey so interesting and enticing that we wish it were true, even as we realize it is not, we discern we are dealing with magical realism, the stuff of the eschaton. The child wins over the live Bengali tiger. He tames him. Pi becomes the alpha male on this little boat. If ever there were a description of taming of the wild creatures it is in the delicate peace fought for and won on this little boat.

All of which brings us to C. S. Lewis, the tame animal storyteller par excellence. His books are full of talking, tame animals. They are real animals, not just allegories or types of humans. Lewis believed that humans were intended to tame the animals, as did Pi, and that there were always

---

1. Martel, *Life of Pi*.

exemplary humans who could do so. Animals were also capable of suffering, and humans in particular should avoid intentionally afflicting suffering on them. Lewis, however, although his mythical heavenly Narnia was full of animals, stopped short of both vegetarianism and a full doctrine of animal salvation.

C. S. LEWIS AND THE ENTWINING OF HUMAN AND ANIMAL

This chapter will examine his omission. Animals and human animals have had a long and fraught relationship. Our collective lives coinhere and are mutually entwining. Can lives so interconnected and similarly embodied on earth be separated in heaven? Should we be vegetarian? What does dominion mean? Why is animal suffering so important for theodicy? In the last part of the chapter I look at the problem of evolution and whether it needs to be understood as *essentially* "red in tooth and claw," and how it makes a difference if it is not.[2]

I will examine C. S. Lewis's, Andrew Linzey's, and Thomas Torrance's arguments (and in passing those related arguments of Michael Lloyd and Christopher Southgate) on animals and salvation, though many other writers are examining this question from different standpoints—Denis Edwards, John Haught, Jürgen Moltmann, Celia Deane-Drummond among others. I argue—with Linzey—that C. S. Lewis does not go far enough in the scope of creaturely redemption. I would agree with him that all arguments in this area are speculative and tentative. I would agree with Lewis and Linzey that the salvation of creatures is tied in some way to the salvation of humanity. Humans must be the restorers of right relationship among the animals, though only as a part of the whole drama of salvation.

Lastly I examine the problem of evolution, not covered by Lewis or Linzey, except in passing. I note that while the problem of evil can hope to deal with evil which seems to work against the overall fabric of goodness evident in creation, God cannot be easily reconciled with a creative process which is inherently fuelled by predation and destruction. I examine recent evolutionary theory and philosophy to see whether evolution needs to be understood this way.

---

2. The ideas in this paper are also discussed in Hoggard Creegan, *Animal Suffering*.

ANIMALS IN THE BIBLE AND IN NARNIA

Although we have read the Bible for a long time without thinking much of animals, when we do look closer they are everywhere. Animals and humans share a day of creation, the sixth day, even if they are distinguished there. The early chapters of Genesis also give us the image of an ark, the sole purpose of which was to save all of life on earth that could be drowned, human and animal alike. To fulfil that purpose of salvation human and animals need to endure a long and intimate journey. Their fates are closely entwined, though the animals are dependent on the care and faithfulness of humans. Animals and humans alike are given every plant to eat until the post-diluvian concession changes that order of things. Even so, at a time when things may have become perilous for animals, they nevertheless come under the Noahic covenant, post flood, further reinforcing the sense of solidarity under God amongst all forms of animal life. Later God defers judgment on Ninevah, in part because of the number of dumb animals. Animals and humans alike share in the curse of the death of the first born, when the angel of death visits Egypt. Animals share with shepherds and visiting astrologers the privilege of witnessing the infant Jesus. A donkey bears his mother to Bethlehem and Jesus to Jerusalem. Jesus wrestles with the wild animals in his desert sojourn. Jesus promises that God knows when a sparrow falls. Lambs will forever be associated with the slain Christ, and when Peter is told to feed the sheep—with those of us in the Body of Christ as well.

Then, most famously of all, there is the image in Isaiah 11:6: The wolf will live with the lamb, the leopard will lie down with the goat, the calf and the lion and the yearling. And in Isaiah 62:25, the lion will eat straw like an ox. This is the image of the peaceable kingdom. Scripture gives eschatological hints, with the eyes of faith, of a huge Chagall tapestry, animals included as actors in every scene, and a dreamlike merging of roles portrayed.

The idea that animals might be a part of the new heavens and the new earth is therefore not completely devoid of all biblical sense, even if we might leave open what exactly the meaning of this salvation might be. Lewis shows this truth in all his Narnia books where animals and humans alike share in the pain of a Narnia under curse, animals and humans equally defend Narnia and Aslan in battle, and come in the end to share the delights of the return of Aslan and the new Narnia. Humans, he says famously, are "between the angels who are our elder brothers and the beasts who are our jesters, servants, and playfellows."[3]

C. S. LEWIS AND THE PROBLEM OF PAIN

For C. S. Lewis the problem of animals is related to cosmic and earthly fallenness. Both humans and animals live in a less than ideal state of connection because something is wrong in the universe. In the past animal suffering, and indeed all suffering and imperfection could be blamed on the human Adamic fall from grace. No longer is that possible. Rather than dismissing all notions of fallenness, or reinterpreting fall in a purely existential sense, Lewis argues for a theology of fallenness that is wider than humanity in scope and origin; humans cannot be responsible for all the disorder in the universe because animals existed for so long before humans. These animals preyed on one another and suffered both pain and real suffering—and became extinct. "The intrinsic evil of the animal world," says Lewis, "lies in the fact that animals, or some animals, live by destroying each other."[4] Taking note of animals as beings somewhere significant on the scale of sentience, capable of suffering and not just passing pain, leads immediately to questions about God's goodness and about animal salvation. This has been resolved by some who insist that animal predation is just God's way of doing things.[5] We have to live by a different code, to be sure, but this does not make God wrong; our imperfect world is in a cosmic sense, the best of all possible worlds. The great values of human sentience and freedom required this carnage. Lewis disagrees with this assessment, as do I.

If animal predation and suffering is a problem, then, what is the theological solution? Human suffering is resolved at one level by noting the benefits of suffering—soul making, character making—and the grace of being one with God through Christ who also suffered for and with us. Humans are compensated by relationship with God and through eternal life. Human freedom is also a theodicy defence. But animals have no similar freedom of choice; they do not know good and evil in a similar way.

A good God could not have intended this. Therefore something outside of God caused this state of affairs. According to Lewis, the only other possibility is the fallenness of angelic powers. He says: "The doctrine of

---

3. Lewis, *That Hideous Strength*, 378.
4. Lewis, *The Problem of Pain*, 423.
5. This is the position of Christopher Southgate in *The Groaning of Creation*.

Satan's existence and fall is not among the things we know to be untrue: it contradicts not the facts discovered by scientists but the mere, vague 'climate of opinion' that we happen to be living in."[6]

Lewis is forthright in giving no weight to the general "climate of opinion" as a guide in any moral matters. He does, however, want to maintain the distinction between humans and the creaturely world, and this he achieves by affirming that animals can be resurrected only if they are the tame animals of humans. Lewis does believe that it was a part of the original mandate for humans that they restore the lack or fallenness in creation. Humans failed to take up their mandate and instead joined the enemy. The boundary between the animal and the human was at the point (given by God) when humans were able to talk about "I."[7] At this point humans had the power of dominion over animals. In Lewis's world all humans would have had the powers of the little boy Pi, able to tame live Bengali tigers at close quarters, or the powers of Francis over the wolves. In Jesus we see the perfect man who exhibits this perfection precisely in his power over creaturely and physical forces, taming wild animals and calming the storm. Lewis adds, speaking from his long love for and proximity to animals:

> Even now more animals than you might expect are ready to adore man if they are given a reasonable opportunity; for man was made to be the priest and even, in one sense, the Christ, of animals—the mediator through whom they apprehend so much of the Divine splendour as their irrational nature allows.[8]

A great deal depends on Lewis's notion of tame animals. He was no doubt influenced by the harmonious households of humans and animals he enjoyed in his own situation. He says, "Atheists [regard] the taming of an animal by a man as a purely arbitrary interference of one species with another. The 'real' or 'natural' animal to them is the wild one, and the tame animal is an artificial or unnatural thing. But a Christian must not think so . . . on the tame animal we must base all our doctrine of beasts."[9]

This is interesting, though obviously controversial. Do we really want to agree that the tamed animal is more worthy than the grand wild specimen so revered by our present day climate of opinion? Lewis would argue that the notion of tameness does not include any diminution of terrible

---

6. Lewis, *The Problem of Pain*, 423.
7. Ibid., 400.
8. Ibid.
9. Ibid., 424–25.

qualities like the roaring of the lion, or presumably, the ability to subsist in wild and untamed territory. The tameness Lewis advocates would be somewhere between that of the domestic cat and the tamed wolf of St Francis. Lewis casts new and interesting light on the story of Knut, and other animals like him. Knut, a polar bear, was born into the Berlin zoo in 2006 (he died at four years old) but abandoned by his mother.[10] One "climate of opinion" regards any interference in the natural state of affairs, where the mother abandoned the newly born infant, as wrong. If humans were to bring up this cub it would be an untenable and unjustifiable interference in a process that is good only if humans are not involved. A view of the world that includes the idea of human dominion would argue that humans have not only the right but the duty to interfere for the sake of the life of the animal.

On the other hand, in 2009 a chimpanzee pet and animal actor named Travis attacked and critically mauled a visitor to its owner. Chimps are hard to domesticate as adults and are four times stronger than the average human. The chimp's owner had disregarded signs that the animal was wild, and at the time of the tragedy the animal had been given Xanax.[11] Travis's owner was living in uneasy equilibrium with this wild animal rather than having truly tamed him. Lewis would argue that taming should never be of a kind that denies an animal its true character, nor should taming be confused with domestication which requires many generations of co-evolution with humans.

Interestingly, all of Lewis's places of refuge and holy places were full of unusual animals—St Anne's and Narnia, for instance. He describes how humans become more human and animals more their God-given selves when they interact with one another; but these are places of eschatological significance, and not just models for how humans should live now. Yet in his imaginative and moral world he anticipated the animal advocates of the next half century and beyond. He would have approved the work of Jane Goodall and Dian Fossey, who are famous for finding companionship with animals in the wild, taming them in so far as day to day interaction and observation is possible, along with a considerable degree of mutual affection. He shares a moral and intellectual worldview with Mark Bekoff, a modern day interpreter of animals in a diverse range of settings. Author of *The Animal Manifesto* and *Wild Justice*, Bekoff makes the case that animals

10. See http://en.wikipedia.org/wiki/Knut_(polar_bear) accessed Sept 21, 2013.
11. see http://en.wikipedia.org/wiki/Travis_(chimpanzee), access Sept 21, 2013.

experience a wide range of emotions and moral reactions, and that they and we can only benefit if we change our behaviour towards them and widen our compassion footprint.[12]

VIVISECTION AND INTERANIMATION

Most important, though, Lewis makes a plea for an end to vivisection and to the deliberate infliction of animal suffering. It is animal suffering that makes Lewis think there might be a heaven for animals, though he also adds that God is not a calculating machine, rewarding a creature in equal measure to the pain in this life.

> The absence of "soul" . . . makes the infliction of pain upon them not easier but harder to justify. For it means that animals cannot deserve pain, nor profit morally by the discipline of pain, nor be recompensed by happiness in another life for suffering in this. Thus all those factors which render pain more tolerable or make it less totally evil in the case of human beings will be lacking in the beasts.[13]

The maintaining of this absence of soul, or of a distinction from humanity, however, is the reason that Lewis is cautious about general animal resurrection, unless perchance the animals have developed a self or soul "in" us. Anticipating—with Alister Hardy—the ecological sensitivities of the half century after his death, Lewis had a very strong concept of interanimation, by which individuals were linked strongly with others by invisible ties. He draws on the constant reference to being "in Christ" in the Gospels, as an example, and he suspects there are other forms of interanimation also.[14] In the Narnia books, for example, the children are constantly referred to as "sons of Adam" and "daughters of Eve." All of this, he thinks, is a form of mystical togetherness we barely understand. Why not extend this notion downward. As we are saved in Christ, so animals might be saved in us.

Lewis's notion of interanimation is interesting because it also was so far ahead of his time. The radical withinness of all life is now much more evident. Not only do we share at a biological level the full apparatus of enzymes and genes and biochemistry and origins in a way that could never

---

12. Bekoff, *The Animal Manifest*; Bekoff and Pierce, *Wild Justice*.
13. Lewis, "Vivisection."
14. Lewis, *The Problem of Pain*, 404.

have been imagined in the 1960s, we also share with higher animals culture and sign making and tool use and creativity.[15] James Lovelock's Gaia hypothesis and Rupert Sheldrake's admittedly controversial understanding of morphic fields add further scientific weight to the idea of the close interconnectedness and solidarity of all life on earth.[16] Lovelock adds weight to this argument by postulating a delicate and interconnecting system of homeostasis, at all levels of life and between all levels of life, with the highest level, Gaia, existing above the level of humans. Sheldrake postulates morphic fields, not unlike magnetic fields, responsible for the direction and "causation" of life at all levels of existence. Lewis, along with a few other idiosyncratic early twentieth century thinkers, was anticipating some of the deep ecological consciousness we now take almost for granted, and was drawing appropriate ethical and metaphysical conclusions.

Lewis, then, introduces the problem of animal suffering, the theodicy problem associated with animals and presses towards animal redemption. He brings these themes to life in his fairy stories—animals are very much a part of the redeemed Narnia—but he leaves the details and the hard lines of the doctrine open. However, Lewis's quick solution to the problem of salvation—that only tame animals are resurrected falls somewhat short of a satisfactory response. It is similar to arguments that only humans who have reached the age of reason, or have been able to respond to others in some way can be saved. Surely this is not divine justice for the poor cat who suffers twice, in being put down instead of tamed, in being denied life, and human companionship and then also salvation? While this solution does nothing for most living animals it similarly does not solve the problem of pre-human animal suffering, which covered and included a vast scale. I will take up the problem of animal salvation later.

T. F. TORRANCE

I want to look briefly now at two theologians who interact with and extend Lewis's argument. The first is Thomas Torrance. Like Lewis he believes in

---

15. There were other contemporaries, however, who also interestingly were of Lewis's persuasion. Most interesting is the work of Alister Hardy, head of the department of zoology at Oxford, who kept his holistic spiritual convictions largely silent, although they were evident in his convictions that ecology and interconnectedness were the way of the future in biology. See Hay, *God's Biologist*.

16. Lovelock, *Gaia*; Sheldrake, *Morphic Resonance*.

a pre-human angelic fall, and specifically because he takes the scientific depiction of "nature red in tooth and claw" seriously. Torrance does not so much point to anything in the world as broken or fallen or demon possessed; rather it is the way different levels are out of sync that he perceives as the result of fallenness. The last few decades have only seen an increase in our awareness of how disordered the overall ecology of the world is, how much it is exacerbated by humans, and how terribly interdependent each form of life is upon all others. Torrance, like Lewis, imagines that the human calling as being, together with creatures, to bring out the hidden surprises of nature, something science can surely be seen to do. Where he extends or makes more explicit the arguments of Lewis is in the subtle interplay of different levels of existence, and in work which humans and the creation were intended to accomplish. Although postulating an alien power of evil at work is never easy nor inherently believable, the idea becomes much more plausible, when like the enemy in the parable of the wheat and the tares, the evil works primarily against the good ordering and interconnections of God's world. Some of this is assumed also in Lewis's snow-locked Narnia. While the wicked powers ruled over Narnia, Spring would never come; even the land was affected by the presence of evil.

Explaining some of the mix of redemption and tragedy that is the human predicament, he says,

> However, when man himself is seized of evil, and his interaction with the Creator is damaged and disordered, his interaction with nature becomes damaged and disordered as well. Something very different takes place, for the whole balance of nature is upset. Man continually infects nature with his own disorder even in the midst of these priestly and redemptive operations.[17]

For Torrance, then, an extra level of fallenness comes to pass when humans are involved. From this stems much of the suffering of animals at human hands. It does not explain, of course, animal predation or extinction many aeons before the emergence of mammals, let alone humanity. Torrance goes on to say that it is in humanity rather than in nature that evil "has lodged itself."[18] And it is in technology that the redemptive and destructive powers of humanity have been magnified. The powers of technology he applies also—as does Jacques Ellul—to the subtle regions of abstract thought.

17. T. F. Torrance, *Divine Contingent Reality*, 130.
18. Ibid.

Drawing on this deep sense that humans can bring good and fruitfulness in and through the created world, Torrance articulates more formally than does Lewis, the notion that humans may have been intended to bring peace and harmony back to the levels of creation; instead humans have perverted and enormously magnified the evil.

There is something very attractive in Torrance's view, and yet I would want to be very hesitant about a theology that almost presents a human fall as a surprise for God. Torrance does bring out the sense in which humans exposed the corruption harbouring in the creation, enormously magnified it, and also made possible the coming of a messiah. The second theologian is the world expert in animal theology and of their causes.

ANDREW LINZEY

Linzey makes a life's work of the insights Lewis applied less systematically. He agrees with Lewis about the animal pain, and about the pre-human fallenness of nature. (Drawing on the work of Michael Lloyd, he does give other possibilities, the fall of the world soul, or the gradual fall of creation as in process theology, but he dismisses these as inadequate.)[19] But he goes much further than Lewis. Linzey affirms Lewis's use of imagination to do theological exploration, his image of the Great Lady, for example, who keeps dogs cats, birds and other animals, tending them all and enabling their kind interconnection.[20]

Where Linzey expands Lewis's arguments is in saying that if cruelty to animals is wrong, then so is eating them:

> Humans can now make a difference in reversing Satanic corruption, by themselves electing to kill and injure as few animals as possible. We are thus able to see Lewis's contention that animals can only be understood in their relationship to human beings as a deeper issue for practical theology. Humans are morally at the centre of creation: as their Fall affects the non-human world so too will their redemption. Since animals are involuntarily tied to human sin, the redemption of humanity matters to the animal world.[21]

---

19. See Lloyd, "Fall."
20. Linzey, "C. S. Lewis' Theology of Animals," 65.
21. Ibid., 77.

Linzey applauds Lewis's theological orthodoxy and the way in which he keeps alive the drama of redemption and the crucial place that animal/human relations have in that drama, while nevertheless steering clear of the deification of nature or of pantheism. The mystery that Lewis, Linzey and Torrance would wish to extract from nature is that of the as yet unchartered connection between animals and humans, rather than the merging of the identity of nature and God. As Linzey says,

> But movements of ecological sensitivity, which otherwise Lewis might have supported, have shown themselves in reaction to be prone to the deification of nature in which, shorn of metaphysical notions, God becomes wholly identified with nature and thus predation itself is baptised as a new natural law. "Whole earth" theologians have singularly failed to address the issue which Lewis squarely faced: the intrinsic evil of animal predation. This omission on the part of the most eco-theologians has compromised a proper regard for animal welfare, not to mention a doctrine of God who is just and holy. Lewis has kept alive a trinitarian tradition sensitive to issues of animal pain while others have ventured into pathways of pantheism and panentheism.[22]

Linzey also expands Lewis's arguments about self and resurrection. Lewis argued that it was only possibly in the development of a self in relationship to human masters that an animal could hope to achieve salvation. Linzey, however, argues that recent scholarship in the area of animals makes it evident that there are higher levels of sentience very close to that of the human already existing in animals.

Many others have ventured into this field. No one of course, knows exactly what a redeemed life for animals would be like, or whether particular animals or just representations of them are present, whether they live in the mind of God, or in a more real way, if indeed anything is more real than the mind of God. But then of course nobody knows about us either. We have no detailed scenario for post-mortem existence, just shadows and images of physical resurrection and joy and peace and the end of earthly corruption.

LEWIS AND CURRENT SCIENCE

Nevertheless Lewis can be seen as a harbinger of and advocate for concerns that were to burst onto the theological consciousness later in the twentieth

22. Ibid., 78.

century. Lewis did not know the detailed work on animals, much of it now obtained from observations in the wild, in the work of Ian Tattersall, Frans De Waal, Dian Fossey, Jane Goodall, and Mike Bekoff, among others. Like many great thinkers Lewis seems to have had intuitions which were prescient. His work is consistent also with the growing ecological consensus; we are all more connected and more dependent than we once knew. Our DNA is shockingly similar to mice and wheat, not massively bigger, as was once supposed. We carry within us the imprint of all stages of life before us. Humans are to be viewed again as more like the microcosm of the middle ages than they have ever been since that time.[23] After decades of observation of animals in their context, in their natural groups and in the wild we now know that they often exhibit signs, grunts and non-verbal signals very like ours. That, together with the sense of connection based around these signs, and the close similarity of animals in terms of origins and DNA gives us reason to think that they feel many of the same emotions we feel, with varying degrees of sentience. Even our highest moral sentiments appear to have deep evolutionary roots. Mirror neurons and von economo neurons—both of which appear to be associated with empathy—give us further reasons to think we are not just anthropomorphising when we read emotions onto higher animals, especially higher primates, elephants, dogs, crows and dolphins. Rather, we may be anthropomorphising in the extent of the exclusion of animal life from the concerns of salvation theology in the last two millennia. The clue of self-recognition in a mirror, which appears to be linked to a sense of self, lends support to the idea that even among the animals there are varying degrees of self-consciousness as well.

Furthermore Lewis's controversial sense of interanimation has surprising resonances in Rupert Sheldrake's work looking at morphic field connections between humans and animals, especially between some sensitive humans and the animals to which they are attached. Furthermore this strange term, interanimation is found resonating through the New Testament. Are we not thought to be "in Christ," and Christ in us. Because this term makes very little sense to us as modern people we do not dwell on it, even if it is promulgated to some extent in liturgy. In all Lewis's books, however, there is a straining towards an understanding of interanimation. In Narnia, Christmas and summer never come because evil is loose in the world. Not until the concept of Gaia from James Lovelock has it been said better, that the actions of humans change the land and its expression.

23. Marilynne Robinson speaks to this in Robinson, *Absence of Mind*, xiii–xv.

C. S. LEWIS, ANIMALS, AND NATURE RED IN TOOTH AND CLAW

Lovelock is expressing a scientific concept, that there are levels of homeostasis above the level of the human; while the prophets and C. S. Lewis are reflecting on the parallel spiritual truth. Humans must enter Narnia, because they have a role, as sons and daughters of Adam and Eve, to bring harmony back to the planet—as they cooperate with and beckon Aslan. And Lewis's trees are remarkable. They are alive, they have spirit within them, and they are intelligent. In modernity we have tended to see trees as just machine-like entities for doing photosynthesis. Only recently the convergent evolution school in biology has suggested that trees are distributed intelligences,[24] an idea also reflected in the science fiction work of Orson Scott Card.[25] Conway Morris sees evolution as perhaps a search engine for consciousness, and that the trees are forms of intelligence we have long overlooked. And in that remarkable and final book, *Till We Have Faces*, Lewis hints at an unseen world behind the surface of our ordinary humdrum world, a world which makes sense of the seemingly meaningless drama of choice we are given, and one which is tied strongly to the proper functioning of nature itself.[26] None of Lewis's world makes sense without these deep connections. He has re-mythologized our world, and the science of the last few decades is beginning to catch up. All of these very close connections, hinted at in Lewis, and affirmed at another level by some scientists, speak very closely to our theology of nature and of redemption.

If animals are so much closer to us than we thought, if animals have been given over to us, if their welfare is in our hands, then at the very least we need to take great care that we do not deliberately harm or neglect animals with higher forms of sentience. Certainly Lewis was right in his anti-vivisection stance, but how do we then justify the eating of meat? I do not think we can read the answer directly from nature, not even our newly understood connection, but the similarity of emotions we see in higher animals must give us pause for thought.

THE QUESTION OF WHAT WE EAT

C. S. Lewis stopped short of a strict vegetarianism. Linzey, however, argues very strongly that the only consistent position for someone who recognizes

---

24. Conway Morris, *The Deep Structure of Convergence*. See especially the chapter by Anthony Trewavas, "Aspects of Plant Intelligence," 68–110.

25. Card, *Xenocide*.

26. Lewis, *Till We Have Faces*.

animal intelligence and dignity is a vegetarian stance. We might note also that there is a growing vegetarian sensitivity, both among Christians and secular people. This is in part fuelled by the recognition that animal farming is more intensive and much less sustainable than is the farming of plants. There are some nutrition experts who claim that a meat free diet is healthier, while others claim exact the opposite, citing the flourishing of Inuit communities who eat almost entirely a meat diet.[27] A desire not to eat animal flesh, however, is also growing as people reflect on the cruelty often associated with animal farming and culling.

I would stop short of arguing strongly for an absolute vegetarianism even though I would see this as some sort of ideal. I take this position for a number of reasons.

1. Whatever we may think of the evolutionary process, and I find predation troubling, the eating of flesh is endemic. It has also been an integral part of the diet of humans for thousands of years, perhaps tens of thousands. While some people can easily adapt a vegetarian diet others cannot do so without suffering depression and ill health. Thus the need for meat is in the biological make-up of many people. I would appeal to the parable of the wheat and tares, that evil is mixed with good to the extent that they cannot always be disentangled. We can't in fact always save ourselves or choose the pure path by our own efforts.

2. There is a moral continuum in meat eating along which we might all place ourselves. Amongst meat eaters there is at one end the American meat machine. Meat is processed by huge often brutal meat killing plants and distributed great distances. Even large animals like cows are kept in crowded dirty booths and fed a mix of nutrients, antibiotics and other additives. At the other end of the spectrum is the story of the American Indian—similar to the stories of many other hunter gatherers—where the buffalo herds were considered to be fellow nations and at the death of an animal God was thanked for the sacrifice of this life. Every part of the animal was harvested. In the present day situation we can edge ourselves as close as possible to the blessed end of the spectrum by buying locally from farmers who keep animals in free range conditions, and kill animals by humane methods.

3. In societies where vegetarianism is not endemic, vegetarians and more especially their children can suffer terrible deficiencies in B12 and

---

27. For advocacy of a strict vegan diet see Esselstyn, *Prevent and Reverse Heart Disease*.

other nutrients. In New Zealand in 2002, a baby died of B12 deficiency when its parents had fed it a vegan diet. The parents were convicted of mistreatment and imprisoned for five years. This is not an isolated case.

4. The parents of children who are allergic or autistic could not possibly keep to a vegetarian diet as well as all the other constraints placed on the child's diet. For them this option would be the last straw in their already harried existence.

5. For Christians, and for many others, eating is not just the taking in of nutrients but also involves a sacramental gathering and interconnection with others. In some situations it is better to join with others in a meal than it is to be a purist about the eating of vegetables only.

6. It can also be argued that many farmers do have relationships of mutual affection with their animals while they are alive, and do care for them and attempt to enhance their lives and to free them from suffering. Perhaps these animal lives, even if they are cut short, count for something in the larger scheme of things.

There is a great deal of work to be done in moving church and society towards a vegetarian norm. Nevertheless I do see the vegetarian option as an ideal, and one towards which we should perhaps be moving as a community and certainly as people of faith.

EVOLUTION

Some of the theodicy confusion concerning animals in the long, long prehistory of humanity emerges because we take on face value that the brutal struggle for survival alone must propel the evolutionary process. The life we have now is only at the cost of absolute death of other "lower" creatures. Evolution, which is indubitably a fact, is nevertheless always couched within a certain "nature red in tooth and claw" metaphysics and it is increasingly obvious that this need not be so.

Surrounding evolution, it is a well-known fact that for the last fifty years or so, give or take a few mavericks, and lesser known schools of thought, evolution has been seen in light of the Central Dogma. Under this paradigm DNA changes protein and not vice versa, and DNA changes only by random fluctuations in an organism which does or does not survive. Nothing drives or guides or pulls the evolutionary process into the future.

There is, however, great heterodoxy in the theory of evolution. There are now a huge number of other approaches to evolution than the ones made popular in the human mind by Richard Dawkins who is always slanting the central dogma of evolution toward one that leads inexorably to the presumption of atheism.[28]

Simon Conway Morris, for instance, argues that constraints and convergence in the evolutionary process provide hints of *telos*, observable even by the scientist.[29] Stuart Kauffman talks of self-organising elements.[30] Sapp describes the theories surrounding deep altruism and cooperation inherent in the evolutionary process at all levels which have persisted in the last one hundred years and are now being discovered and validated in more detail. Epigenesis has sprung into the scientific literature with all its much more fluid understanding of environment and heredity, and Philip Ball has described the way in which much of the evolutionary process is dependent upon and reveals the deep physics and chemistry beneath it.[31] Many others have argued for an emergent, multi-layered view of life in which every level requires its own laws and grammar.[32] All these newer dynamics point to a process which is guided from below by deep inner principles of life—suggestive perhaps of *logos*. The mystery of life itself is suggestive of the constant upholding of being in a dimension at "right angles" to our present existence. Thus God works from below and more actively to uphold all that exists, without in any sense cancelling the freedom, nor the apparent randomness and indeed historical contingency of parts of the process of evolution. What matters to theology here is that the process is not at heart one of randomness, driven only by the ever pressing will to survive and dominate others. There are deeper, more loving, gentler aspects at work which can be seen to set the direction of the evolutionary process. This makes more possible a reconciliation of evolutionary theory with theological impulses which affirm the salvation of humans and of creatures as the *telos* or end of history.

If there are deep constraints, working at the level of natural law, as strong and as constraining as gravity and the weak and strong nuclear forces, then we are dealing with a very different metaphysical beast in the evolutionary process. Then evolution becomes a process which can be seen

---

28. See, for instance, Sapp, *Genesis*, in which the history of evolutionary thought is detailed.
29. Conway Morris, *Life's Purpose*.
30. Kauffmann, *Investigations*.
31. Carey, *The Epigenetics Revolution*; Ball, *Shapes, Nature's Patterns*.
32. See for instance, Klapwijk, *Purpose in the Living World*.

to be deeply beautiful and at the same time to have fallen and corruptible aspects and directions. Then it is more possible to see that there might be final causes working alongside the efficient and material causes in nature.

John Haught, in a recent work, has urged us to note that evolution can be seen in this multi-layered way, that scientific explanations need not exhaust the possibilities for explanation of a biological event.[33] Nevertheless offering explanations at several different levels only works if the explanations do not contradict one another or cancel one another out. Natural selection by blind mutation has always had a grammar very different from that of the indwelling logos and life breathing Spirit. Newer understandings of evolution may break this deep incompatibility and open up a way to seeing final causes as a not incoherent way of understanding the evolutionary process. In this way, although theology is not directly adding to science, it is contributing to the sense or meaning of the picture science presents.

CONCLUSION

Humans and animals are just beginning to know one other. In the past there have been many odd notions of animals, that they are just machines, or that humans and animals are made of different metaphysical stuff. Even today it is Roman Catholic orthodoxy that humans have a separate ensouling at the edge of the emerging species that is homo sapiens. We are beginning to discover both our uniqueness and our similarities to animals. Humans are also recognizing the extent of the bonds of sympathy and intelligence between ourselves and other creatures, a sympathy that is only increased by the knowledge of humanity's long birthing through 4 billion years of evolutionary history. When Pi settled down to life on the boat with his tiger, he found himself pleased of the company, disgruntled though it was. Humans and animals have had these relationships for as long as human history but we are only just beginning to recognize their depth. C. S. Lewis was way ahead of his time in championing the rights of animals, and especially in championing the problem of their suffering and their place in the moral order of the universe.

---

33. Haught, "Evolution and the Suffering of Sentient Life after Darwin."

7

Mere Christianity for Mere Gods

Lewis on Theosis[1]

MYK HABETS

WALKING IN MIRABILIBUS SUPRA ME

IN HIS ESSAY "TRANSPOSITION," after speaking about the Incarnation, Lewis makes the comment: "But I walk in *mirabilibus supra me* and submit all to the verdict of real theologians."[2] While Lewis is unclear as to what constitutes a "real theologian," I have taken his offer up and in this chapter discuss the contours of what a Lewis-inspired doctrine of theosis looks like. In this venture too we all walk "in things too wonderful for us"![3] Having said that, we can and must say something, despite the apophatic reticence

---

1. An earlier version of this essay was published as Habets, "Walking *in mirabilibus supra me*: How C. S. Lewis Transposes Theosis," *Evangelical Quarterly: An International Review of Bible and Theology in Defence of the Historic Christian Faith* 82 no.1 (January, 2010), 15–27.

2. Lewis, "Transposition," 83. Lewis often distinguished himself from "real theologians," as for instance in the preface to *Mere Christianity*, vi.

3. This is a slight misquotation of Ps 131.1 in the Vulgate, where the Psalmist says that he is not proud, and he does not occupy himself "with things too wonderful for me" (Latin: *in mirabilibus supra me*). I am grateful to my colleague Dr. George Wieland for this insight.

characteristic of all Christian theology, about the mystery of salvation. It is the mysterious nature of salvation which makes the concept of theosis so attractive to Lewis and indeed, to others of us.

In recent decades the doctrine of theosis, once a theological *bête noire*, has undergone a radical popularity shift and is now the toast of the Western theological guild. Doctrines of theosis now find their way into mainstream treatments in biblical theology, such as Michael Gorman's *Inhabiting the Cruciform God*, through to works of western systematic theology, such as my own attempts at "Reforming theosis" on the soil of Reformation theology.[4] So fecund have such studies been on theosis that it has provoked Eastern Orthodox scholars into a reaction—not much of it being very positive. In recommending a short work by Norman Russell, Peter Bouteneff identifies and labels much recent talk on theosis as "facile, over-spiritualized, or abstract."[5] Bouteneff also makes the point that theosis expresses a relation, not a thing; a point lost on many contemporary apologists for a doctrine of divinization. Themes and doctrines of theosis are now ubiquitous in works by the Orthodox,[6] Lutherans,[7] Roman Catholicism,[8] Anglicanism,[9] Evangelicalism,[10] and Reformed theology.[11] The many reasons for the recovery of theosis in recent thought need not detain us here;[12]

---

4. Something a number of detractors are obviously not happy about! See my "Reforming Theosis"; *Theosis in the Theology of Thomas Torrance*; "Reformed Theosis?"; and "Theosis, Yes; Deification, No,"; McCormack, "For Us and Our Salvation"; "What's at Stake"; "Participation in God, Yes, Deification, No"; and Jonathan Slater, "Salvation as Participation."

5. Bouteneff, "Foreword," 11.

6. Foundational texts here include: Stavropoulos, *Partakers of the Divine Nature*; Lossky, *The Mystical Theology of the Eastern Church*; Mantzaridis, *The Deification of Man*; and Nellas, *Deification in Christ*. Russell points out that before the 1960s the average Orthodox Christian would not have known what the term *theosis* referred to, it being a technical term familiar only to monks and patristic scholars.

7. One thinks here of the Manermaa School; see Braaten and Jenson, *Union with Christ*.

8. For instance, Meconi, "Deification in the Thought of John Paul II"; and Keating, *Deification and Grace*.

9. For an overview see Allchin, *Participation in God*.

10. See Clendenin, *Eastern Orthodox Christianity*.

11. In addition to works already cited see Murphy, "Reformed Theosis?"

12. Russell, *Fellow Workers with God*, 14, identifies four crucial factors: (1) the rediscovery of the theology of St Gregory Palamas, (2) the impact of Russian religious philosophy, (3) the recovery of the spirituality of the *Philokalia*, and (4) the reengagement of Orthodox scholars with the early Greek Fathers. See further in Bowron, "Eastern

we merely note the fact that, amongst other factors, there was a renaissance of Eastern Orthodox literature flooding into the West in French and English translation, due in large measure to the Russian diaspora following the Bolshevik revolution. Lewis, a renaissance man in Oxford and Cambridge, was one of the many recipients of this diaspora, and hence he was exposed to doctrines and themes of theosis which worked their way into his own thought and theology.

The sense that there is more to human life than mere existence, more to pleasure than a fleeting sensation, and more to reality than we currently experience, pervades the works of Lewis. As one follower of Lewis has written, "Lewis was a scholar, Oxford don, and international celebrity, but he was above all a man aware of the love and longing inherent in our restless souls. He adored fellowship and laughter and the diversity of human connection (the "four loves," as he called them) that offers but a glimpse of the greater Connection we all seek."[13] As a theological concept, theosis offers Lewis but one way to approximate this sense of longing, connection, and ultimate communion inherent in a Christian soteriology. How to articulate such a doctrine, however, has proven difficult.

Lewis strove, throughout his career, to expound what he knew as "mere Christianity." The concept and the words "mere Christianity" were not original to Lewis, of course, having their roots in earlier Anglican thought.[14] In the sixteenth-century, Richard Hooker, one of Lewis's most adored theologians, masterfully developed the notion of a "mere Christianity" that conformed to the vision of the newly established Anglican Church. Hooker was not striving for the "true Church" in Anglicanism, but rather sought to establish Anglicanism as a faithful but local expression of the body of Christ; a "mere Church" affirming a "mere Christianity" if you will. Of Hooker's masterwork, *Of the Laws of Ecclesiastical Polity*, Lewis had this to say:

> Hooker had never heard of a religion called Anglicanism. He would never have dreamed of trying to "convert" any foreigner to the Church of England. It was to him obvious that a German or Italian would not belong to the Church of England, just as an Ephesian or Galatian would not have belonged to the Church of Corinth.

Promises"; and Habets, "Theosis, Yes; Deification, No."

13. McCracken, "Foundations Mission."
14. Griffin, "What Is Mere Christianity?"

MERE CHRISTIANITY FOR MERE GODS

> Hooker is never seeking for "the true Church," never crying, like Donne, "show me, deare Christ, thy spouse." For him no such problem existed. If by "the Church" you mean the mystical Church (which is partly in Heaven), then of course, no man can identify her. But if you mean the visible Church, then we all know her. She is "a sensibly known company" of all those throughout the world who profess one Lord, one faith, and one Baptism.[15]

The words "mere Christianity" were not original to Lewis either. In the seventeenth-century Richard Baxter, another Anglican divine and favourite of Lewis, used the words "mere Christianity" in *The Saints' Everlasting Rest*. Lewis began making the words "mere Christianity" his own for the first time in print in his introduction to St. Athanasius, *On the Incarnation*. "The only safety is to have a standard of plain, central Christianity ('mere Christianity' as Baxter called it) which puts the controversies of the moment in their proper perspective."[16] Later he writes, "Measured against the ages 'mere Christianity' turns out to be no insipid interdenominational transparency, but something positive, self-consistent, and inexhaustible."[17] The most well-known use of the phrase comes from the 1952 publication of that name for the collected BBC Radio talks of 1943–44.[18] In the preface to *Mere Christianity*, Lewis gives a succinct definition:

> Ever since I became a Christian I have thought that the best, perhaps the only, service I could do for my unbelieving neighbours was to explain and defend the belief that has been common to nearly all Christians at all times. . . . For I am not writing to expound something I call "my religion," but to expound "mere" Christianity, which is what it is and was what it was long before I was born and whether I like it or not.[19]

---

15. Lewis, *English Literature*, 454. For more on the relationship of Lewis to Hooker see Allchin, *Participation in God*, 7–14. Allchin sees the link between the two men not only in terms of "mere Christianity," but also in their doctrines of theosis.

16. Lewis, introduction to *Athanasius on the Incarnation*, 4.

17. Ibid., 6. Not coincidently, this work is where Athanasius makes his famous statement that "The Son of God became a man to enable men to become sons of God." Athanasius, *On the Incarnation*, 340–41.

18. The three broadcast talks were published in three books: *The Case for Christianity*, published in England under the title *Broadcast Talks* (1943), *Christian Behaviour* (1943), and *Beyond Personality* (1944).

19. Lewis, *Mere Christianity*, vi.

In his exposition of mere Christianity Lewis repeatedly turns to those who have preceded him for guidance, the recent past in Anglicanism (Hooker and Baxter for example), and the more distant past in the Doctors of the Church (Athanasius and Augustine, for example). Lewis sought to represent the Great Tradition by mining it for resources and then creatively expressing these thoughts for another generation. Theosis is one such resource Lewis receives and then passes on.

Theosis is largely synonymous with another term *theopoiēsis*. Literally, theosis means "becoming god," and *theopoiēsis*, "making divine" or "making into a god."[20] In English theosis is often expressed by the terms "deification" and/or "divinization."[21] The use of theosis has a rich pedigree extending back through the early church to Scripture itself.[22] While mostly associated with the Greek patristic theologians and Eastern Orthodoxy, theosis also has a developed use in Anglicanism in the west, as Lewis was well aware. In his useful introduction Arthur Allchin looks at the doctrine of theosis as it is to be found in representative Anglican theologians during the last four centuries and in the process uncovers a surprisingly rich heritage in theologians as diverse as Richard Hooker, John Henry Newman, Edward B. Pusey, and Lewis.[23] These Anglican thinkers sought to recover a patristic doctrine of theosis which speaks of a real participation between God and humanity in the work of redemption and sanctification.

When we turn specifically to the work of Lewis we find a veritable saturation of theotic language and concepts. Lewis's treatment of theosis ranges from the explicit to the implicit but it is never far from his sight. Throughout *Mere Christianity* Lewis speaks in the language of theosis on numerous occasions in order to express the ineffable mystery and magnitude of life in union with Christ. Early in the work we read, "If I find in myself a desire which no experience in this world can satisfy, the most probable explanation is that I was made for another world."[24] Not content with this ambiguity we later read that

20. Lampe, *A Patristic Greek Lexicon*, 649.

21. I make no effort to create specialized classifications for these terms but rather treat them as largely synonymous for our purposes here.

22. For recent overviews see Mosser, "The Earliest Patristic Interpretations"; Glazov, "Theosis, Judaism, and Old Testament Anthropology"; Finlan, "Second Peter's Notion of Divine Participation"; and Russell, *The Doctrine of Deification*, esp. 333–44.

23. Allchin, *Participation in God*. Also Newey ("The Form of Reason"), who examines the doctrine of participation and theosis in seventeenth-century Anglican theology.

24. Lewis, *Mere Christianity*, 108.

MERE CHRISTIANITY FOR MERE GODS

> [S]ome people think that after this life, or perhaps after several lives, human souls will be "absorbed" into God. But when they try to explain what they mean, they seem to be thinking of our being absorbed into God as one material thing absorbed into another. . . . If this is what happens to us, then being absorbed is the same as ceasing to exist. It is only the Christians who have any idea of how human souls can be taken into the life of God and yet remain themselves—in fact, very much more themselves than they were before. . . . The whole purpose for which we exist is to be thus taken into the life of God.[25]

If that were not clear enough then later still Lewis expresses his doctrine of theosis with the aid of Scripture (Jn 10.34, citing Ps 82.6):

> [God said] that we were "gods" and He is going to make good His words. If we let Him—for we can prevent Him, if we choose—He will make the feeblest and filthiest of us into a god or goddess, a dazzling, radiant, immortal creature, pulsating all through with such energy and joy and wisdom and love as we cannot now imagine, a bright stainless mirror which reflects back to God perfectly (though, of course, on a smaller scale) His own boundless power and delight and goodness. The process will be long and in parts very painful; but that is what we are in for. Nothing less. He meant what He said.[26]

In 1942, Lewis preached a sermon in the Church of St Mary the Virgin, Oxford, titled "The Weight of Glory," in which he stated in unmistakable terms his affirmation of theosis.

> It is a serious thing to live in a society of possible gods and goddesses, to remember that the dullest and most uninteresting person you talk to may one day be a creature which, if you saw it now, you would be strongly tempted to worship. . . . There are no ordinary people. You have never talked to a mere mortal. . . . But it is immortals whom we joke with, work with, marry, snub, and exploit—immortal horrors or everlasting splendours.[27]

---

25. Ibid., 127–28.
26. Ibid., 162.
27. Lewis, "The Weight of Glory," 101–2. The quotation continues: "or else a horror and a corruption such as you now meet, if at all, only in a nightmare. All day long we are, in some degree, helping each other to one or other of these destinations."

Put more succinctly, he writes, "We want something else which can hardly be put into words—to be united with the beauty we see, to pass into it, to receive it into ourselves, to bathe in it, to become part of it."[28]

Earlier still, in the 1940s Lewis writes, "And we must mean by that fulfilling, precisely, of our humanity; not our transformation into angels nor absorption into Deity. For though we shall be 'as the angels' and made 'like unto' our Master, I think this means 'like with the likeness proper to men': as different instruments that play the same air but each in its own fashion."[29]

Lewis is clear here, as elsewhere, to distinguish a Christian doctrine of theosis from a neo-Platonic notion of absorption, and equally, to guard Christianity from mythic connotations of apotheosis. This is confirmed when in the same work he writes, "'We know not what we shall be'; but we may be sure we shall be more, not less, than we were on earth."[30] This "more not less" principle is central to a Christian doctrine of theosis and Lewis is clear to keep this in mind. "Morality is indispensable," writes Lewis, "but the Divine Life, which gives itself to us and which calls us to be gods, intends for us something in which morality will be swallowed up. We are to be remade . . . and then, surprisingly, we shall find underneath it all a thing we have never yet imagined: a real man, an ageless god, a son of God, strong, radiant, wise, beautiful, and drenched in joy?"[31] In a much later work and in a very different frame of mind Lewis is no less clear on the god-like destiny of humanity, despite the struggle to see how it may come about, when in *A Grief Observed* he almost laments the fact that God's "grand enterprise" is: "To make an organism which is also a spirit; to make that terrible oxymoron, a 'spiritual animal.' To take a poor primate, a beast with nerve-endings all over it, a creature with a stomach that wants to be filled, a breeding animal that wants its mate, and say, 'Now get on with it. Become a god.'"[32]

It is clear that according to Lewis, as for the Patristic sources from which he derives his doctrine of theosis, human gods are distinct from, and different to God himself. Screwtape even knows this when he affirms that God "wants a world full of beings united to Him but still distinct."[33]

28. Ibid., 99.
29. Lewis, "Transposition," 80.
30. Ibid., 81.
31. Lewis, "Man or Rabbit?," 72.
32. Lewis, *A Grief Observed*, 61.
33. Lewis, *The Screwtape Letters*, 38.

These select quotations illustrate a point made by Walter Hooper who, writing in 1966, commented that if there existed a Complete Works of C. S. Lewis and "one were to read from start to finish all the volumes called "Religious Writings" he would, I think, be struck by what I consider the central premise of all Lewis's theological works—a premise implicit, even, in his books on other subjects. It is that all men are immortal."[34] This seems accurate to me. For Lewis, all people are bound for immortality, not the sloughing off of human nature but a participation in the triune Godhead. In *Mere Christianity* he categorically states: "Now the whole offer which Christianity makes is this: that we can, if we let God have His way, come to share in the life of Christ . . . Christ is the Son of God. If we share in this kind of life we also shall be sons of God."[35]

TRANSPOSITION CAN DO ANYTHING!

That Lewis has a doctrine of theosis is clear.[36] Exactly how he conceives the dynamics of theosis is less clear.[37] I propose reading his notion of "Transposition" in tandem with theosis will shed some light on this issue, after all, as Lewis stated in his now famous sermon of the same name, preached in Mansfield College, Oxford in the early 1940s, "in a sense Transposition can do anything."[38] Transposition is a relatively easy concept to grasp; it is to cause two or more things to change places with each other, or to transfer to a different place or context.[39] The connection with a doctrine of theosis is natural. God transposes human being into the divine being without

---

34. Hooper, "Preface," vii.

35. Lewis, *Mere Christianity*, 139–40.

36. According to Knickerbocker, "The Myth That Saves," "In his Christian writings, whatever the literary genre, Lewis's understanding of soteriology is cast in the language of theosis."

37. All arguments to date attempting to make Lewis's doctrine of theosis compatible with Mormonism's doctrine of divinization have failed to make a compelling case. See a survey of the literature and a rebuttal of the claim that Lewis is a "crypto-Mormon" by Passantino, "Are We Destined to Be Gods and Goddesses?" Due to Lewis's insistence on the "irreducible ontological distinction" between God and humans, Jensen ("Shine Like the Son") rightly dismisses all appeals to make Lewis's work compatible with Neoplatonism, Hinduism, Mormonism, or even certain strands of Christian mysticism.

38. Lewis, "Transposition," 84. For other treatments of Transposition see Bramlett, "Transposition"; Hinton, "Transposition," 409; and Mitchell, "Transposition."

39. For a good survey of the concept of Transposition and critical interaction with it, in relation to tongues, see Richie, "Transposition and Tongues."

destroying the human being (or the divine) in the process. God has the ability to translate human existence into the sphere of his own existence.[40] As Lewis prefers to state it:

> You can say that by Transposition our humanity, senses and all, can be made the vehicle of beatitude. Or you can say that the heavenly bounties by Transposition are embodied during this life in our temporary experience. But the second way is the better. It is the present life which is the diminution, the symbol, the etiolated, the (as it were) "vegetarian" substitute. If flesh and blood cannot inherit the Kingdom, that is not because they are too solid, too gross, too distinct, too "illustrious with being." They are too flimsy, too transitory, too phantasmal.[41]

Taking the Incarnation as his starting point, Lewis prefers the downward reference of Transposition, from the divine to the human, although he does not rule out its upward return. Lewis illustrates his emphasis on the downward orientation of Transposition with the statement that "we are told in one of the creeds that the Incarnation worked 'not by conversion of the Godhead into flesh, but by taking of the Manhood into God.'"[42] Lewis then combines Transposition with theosis immediately after this when he concludes, "It seems to me that there is a real analogy between this and what I have called Transposition: that humanity, still remaining itself, is not merely counted as, but veritably drawn into, Deity."[43]

In *Miracles* Lewis further articulates this principle, namely: "the power of the Higher, just in so far as it is truly Higher, to come down, the power of the greater to include the less."[44] Thus the "Grand Miracle" is the Incarnation—the eternal Son becoming man without ceasing to be God. According to Lewis, God descended into humanity so that he could re-ascend and bring with him the precious thing which occasioned the descent—humanity. In order to illustrate this Lewis turns to nature: "It must belittle itself into something hard, small and deathlike, it must fall into the ground: thence the new life re-ascends."[45] This applies to vegetable and

---

40. This is the difference, argues Lewis, between human *bios* from human *zoe*; Lewis, *Mere Christianity*, 126, 139.

41. Lewis, "Transposition," 81–82. Lewis develops this latter point tremendously in his allegory, *The Great Divorce*.

42. Ibid., 83.

43. Ibid.

44. Lewis, *Miracles*, 115.

45. Ibid.,116.

animal life. Amidst this discussion Lewis draws, again, upon the theme of Transposition to explain what is going on. He writes, "All the instances of [this principle] which I have mentioned turn out to be but transpositions of the Divine theme into a minor key."[46]

Lewis sees the purpose of creation as being to improve or develop: "God, from the first, created her (earth) such as to reach her perfection by a process of time."[47] The same goes for the human: "For God is not merely mending, not simply restoring a status quo. Redeemed humanity is to be something more glorious than unfallen humanity would have been, more glorious than any unfallen race now is.... And this super-added glory will, with true vicariousness, exalt all creatures and those who have never fallen will thus bless Adam's fall."[48] Lest he be misunderstood, the "development" of which Lewis speaks is not a natural one, conducive, say, to a theory of evolution.[49] Rather, the development of which Lewis speaks is what in theology would be called theosis—involving justification, sanctification, and finally, glorification. Within his works however, the stress of theosis seems clearly to be on this final aspect—glorification.[50]

In his magisterial sermon "The Weight of Glory,"[51] Lewis discusses the nature of the glory that is to be experienced when the believer is glorified, and it is worthy of extensive quotation:

46. Ibid.

47. Ibid., 125. In "The Weight of Glory," 90–92, 99–100, Lewis develops the same thing, stating that the earth as it currently exists is not our home, not the place to fulfil all our desires. Not yet at least.

48. Ibid., 127. Lewis goes on to favourably discuss what is known as the Scotistic hypothesis—that there would have been an incarnation irrespective of the fall. He also develops the idea throughout his science fiction trilogy. For a discussion of possible worlds semantics see Habets, "On Getting First Things First."

49. Lewis puts the axe to this concept in "The Funeral of a Great Myth." On Lewis's critique of developmentalism see Knickerbocker, "The Myth That Saves," who notes that "The Christian Myth is a Creation-Fall-Redemption-Consummation myth, while the contemporary Western myth is a Creation-Fulfilment myth, which is manifested in many variant expressions, from Social Darwinism to Marxism, imperialism, racism, materialism, and the cult of self-fulfilment."

50. Jensen, "Shine Like the Son," notes the stress throughout *Mere Christianity* on three main ways to achieve theosis: baptism, belief, and Holy Communion. In his other works Lewis stresses the corporate aspect of theosis, the centrality of human free will, the painful process of transformation and the humility that results from the journey. While Jensen is partially correct, the stress throughout Lewis's works is always on what we shall become rather than on how we shall achieve it.

51. This sermon was preached to one of the largest modern crowds ever to assemble

> And this brings me to the other sense of glory—glory as brightness, splendour, luminosity. We are to shine as the sun, we are to be given the Morning Star. I think I begin to see what it means. In one way, of course, God has given us the Morning Star already: you can go and enjoy the gift on many fine mornings if you get up early enough. What more, you may ask, do we want? Ah, but we want so much more—something the books on aesthetics take little notice of. But the poets and the mythologies know all about. We do not want merely to see beauty, though, God knows, even that is bounty enough. We want something else which can hardly be put into words—to be united with the beauty we see, to pass into it, to receive it into ourselves, to bathe in it, to become part of it . . . if we take the imagery of Scripture seriously, if we believe that God will one day give us the Morning Star and cause us to put on the splendour of the sun, then we may surmise that both the ancient myths and the modern poetry, so false as history, may be very near the truth as prophecy.[52]

Use of such analogies as glory, brightness, splendour, and luminosity in the context of soteriology, in particular the eschatological dimensions of such, place this discussion into the sphere of theosis language.[53] We see this, for instance, in Thomas Torrance's use of the analogy of light, and it may be instructive to see how he articulates the idea. According to Torrance the incarnation shows us what true humanity is; it reveals what true "seeing" or "knowing" God consists of,[54] for it is an accurate reflection of the uncreated Light in a created human subject.[55] Torrance contends:

> Jesus was completely and absolutely transparent with the Light of God. . . . Far from being less human because of that, he was more human than any other, indeed perfectly human, for with him the divine Light which is the source of all human life and light had its perfect way. . . . The union between his human life

---

at the Church of St. Mary the Virgin in Oxford.

52. Lewis, "The Weight of Glory," 99–100.

53. Elsewhere Lewis uses other terms to express his doctrine of theosis, including being "in Christ," becoming "new creatures," or sharing in the "glory of God"; as well as with literary images such as the celestial light, the face, the dance, the fountain, the marriage, the winged horse, an infection, and the statue-come-to-life. See Jensen, "Shine Like the Son."

54. Jesus Christ is both "luminous Word" and "audible Light." Torrance, *Christian Theology and Scientific Culture*, 101.

55. This corresponds well with the characterization to saints in heaven as the "Bright People" in *The Great Divorce*, first mentioned on page 29 and many times thereafter.

and the humanising Light of the Creator was unbroken, so that it is through him that the eternal uncreated Light of God shines through to us.[56]

"Transparency" in this discussion functions as an analogy for theosis in the same way as Lewis's use of "glory" functions as such. To experience theosis is to become in a sense transparent or glorious. The goal of theosis is to reflect God's uncreated Light fully and completely, without spot or blemish. The Incarnate Son of God is the Light of God and the Light of the world and it is only as one is united to this Light that one can apprehend it, reflect it, and be light oneself. As Torrance explains: "Since it is in this enlightening and saving Life of the crucified and risen Jesus that the eternal Light and Life of God himself are mediated to us in a form in which we can share in death as well as life, it is through union and communion with Jesus that we are enabled to see the invisible God and live."[57]

According to Lewis, the "weight of glory" carries two connotations, both of which are integral to his doctrine of theosis: luminosity, and fame. Luminosity describes the participation of human creatures into the Divine life (2 Cor 3.18), fame refers to the recognition and joyous reception human creatures receive when united to Christ (Lk 15.7). Jensen reminds us that "one of Lewis's favorite ways to describe this glorious acceptance by God was through the image of the dance, which hints at the order, love, and festivity of heaven."[58] The image of participating in the Divine Dance is of course a clear reference to Patristic and Eastern Orthodox writers on the divine perichoresis and human deification.[59]

To further explicate the notion of Transposition, especially as it relates to theosis, we must turn to another of Lewis's essays, "Meditation in a Toolshed."[60] In this essay Lewis explains how to transpose from the lower level of things to the higher. In short this involves looking "at" something and then looking "along" it. This basically entails the ability to look beyond

---

56. Torrance, *Christian Theology and Scientific Culture*, 96.

57. Ibid., 99.

58. Jensen, "Shine Like the Sun." Jensen cites *Mere Christianity*, 138–40 and notes how often Lewis ends his work with the image of the Divine dance (e.g. *The Problem of Pain, Perelandra*).

59. See for example, Meyendorff, "Theosis in the Eastern Christian Tradition," 475; Cross, "Perichoresis, Deification, and Christological Predication in John of Damascus," 69–124; Otto, "The Use and Abuse of Perichoresis in Recent Theology"; and Choufrine, *Gnosis, Theophany, Theosis*.

60. Lewis, "Meditation in a Toolshed."

a fact (looking at a thing) to seeing the meaning of a thing (looking along it). To illustrate he uses the sunbeam visible through the crack in his toolshed door, a young girl in love, the thinking of a mathematician, a dancing savage, an anthropologist, and a little girl crying over her broken doll. As Lewis observed himself, "When you have got into the habit of making this distinction [between looking at something and looking along it] you will find examples of it all day long."[61]

When applied to human nature we see the usefulness of this distinction for a doctrine of theosis. If one simply looks at a human one may only see a biological entity; nothing but this brute fact. The ability to look along human nature, however, leads to the contemplation of such concepts as the *imago Dei* and then to the Creator God. At that point they will be able to apprehend how humans created in the *imago Dei* are fitted for immortality and ultimately, for participation in God. This helps to explain how and why Lewis refers to all people as potential gods and goddesses. To speak in such a way is not to be taken literally but, when transposed, means that humans are godlike, or, to be more specific, Christ-like. Transposition may only be understood, contends Lewis, from the higher to the lower medium:

> The brutal man never can by analysis find anything but lust in love; the Flatlander never can find anything but flat shapes in a picture; physiology never can find anything in thought except twitchings of the grey matter. It is no good browbeating the critic who approaches a Transposition from below. On the evidence available to him his conclusion is the only one possible.[62]

Lewis concludes, "Everything is different when you approach the Transposition from above."[63] Thus, to transpose the idea of humans as "gods" is not to redefine divinity in terms of anthropology but the other way round. Anthropology is properly speaking a sub-specie under God, relatively speaking; humans are *imago Dei*! As with any distinctively Christian doctrine of theosis, Lewis is clear throughout his writings to uphold the impassible gulf that exists between Creator and creature; between God and humans. In *Mere Christianity*, for instance, he affirms that "What God begets is God; just as what man begets is man. What God creates is not God; just as what man creates is not man. That is why men are not Sons of God in the sense that Christ is. They may be like God in certain ways, but

---

61. Ibid., 52.
62. Lewis, "Transposition," 77.
63. Ibid.

they are not things of the same kind. They are more like statues or pictures of God."⁶⁴ In *The Problem of Pain* he writes, "For we are only creatures; our role must be that of patient to agent . . . mirror to light, echo to voice. Our highest activity must be response, not initiative."⁶⁵ Nor does this mean the same as to say "God is human," unless we are referring to the specific case of the Incarnation and even then this is imprecise language at best. As Lewis closes *The Problem of Pain* he includes a clear and compelling comparison between God and humans:

> As our Earth is to all the stars, so are we men and our concerns to all creation; as all the stars are to space itself, so are all creatures, all thrones and powers and mightiest of the created gods, to the abyss of the self-existing Being, who is to us Father and Redeemer and indwelling Comforter, but of whom no man nor angel can say nor conceive what He is in and for himself, or what is the work that he "maketh from the beginning to the end." For they are all derived and unsubstantiated things. Their vision fails them and they cover their eyes from the intolerable light of utter actuality, which was and is and shall be, which never could have been otherwise, which has no opposite.⁶⁶

The doctrine of theosis in the works of Lewis is understandable only when the method of Transposition is clearly understood. Instead of looking at the thing (the human), one must look along it (to Jesus Christ the *imago Dei*) in order to see how humans really can be godlike. Transposition is thus one way in which Lewis can posit human participation in the Divine nature, without risk of constructing one more myth among the many of human history.⁶⁷

---

64. Lewis, *Mere Christianity*, 124. Lewis ends this discussion with another reference to theosis: "And that is precisely what Christianity is all about. This world is a great sculptor's shop. We are the statues and there is a rumour going round the shop that some of us are some day going to come to life" (126).

65. Lewis, *The Problem of Pain*, 389.

66. Ibid., 153–54. In Passantino's essay, "Are We Destined to Be Gods and Goddesses?," we are also pointed to Lewis's science fiction trilogy *Out of the Silent Planet*, *Perelandra*, and *That Hideous Strength* for more examples of the "impassable gulf between the only Creator and His creatures."

67. For Lewis's defence of Christianity over opposing "myths" see Knickerbocker, "The Myth That Saves." When referring to Christianity Lewis uses "myth" in the Socratic sense of "a not unlikely tale." See Lewis, *The Problem of Pain*, 400.

THE PROBLEM OF PAIN

Earlier we noted Lewis's indication that the process of theosis would be a painful one. We find an allusion to this "painful" process of theosis in the example of the (initially) very annoying Eustace Clarence Scrubb ("and he almost deserved it"),[68] who in *The Voyage of the Dawn Treader* "had turned into a dragon while he was asleep. Sleeping on a dragon's hoard with greedy, dragonish thoughts in his heart."[69] However, captive in his dragon state and after trying to remove the scales himself, Eustace finally learnt to trust Aslan to do the painful task of changing him from a dragon back into a boy—but a transformed boy.

> Then the lion said . . . "You will have to let me undress you." I was afraid of his claws, I can tell you, but I was pretty nearly desperate now. So I just lay flat down on my back to let him do it. The very first tear he made was so deep that I thought it had gone right into my heart. And when he began pulling the skin off, it hurt worse than anything I've ever felt. . . . Then he caught hold of me—I didn't like that much for I was very tender underneath now that I'd no skin on—and threw me into the water. It smarted like anything but only for a moment. After that it became perfectly delicious.[70]

Here we find a vivid illustration of the transposing effect of theosis—something Nellas and other Orthodox writers refer to as Christification.[71] We are also reminded at chapters end that: "It would be nice, and fairly true, to say that 'from that time forth Eustace was a different boy.' To be strictly accurate, he began to be a different boy. He had relapses. . . . The cure had begun."[72] One cannot but think of the promise of the New Covenant spoken of in Ezekiel 36:26–27: "Moreover, I will sprinkle clean water on you, and you will be clean; I will cleanse you from all your filthiness

---

68. Lewis, *Dawn Treader*, 7.

69. Ibid., 73. A similar degrading transformation happens to Rabadash who, after calling down the curse of Tash upon the Narnians, Archenlandians, and Aslan himself, was turned into the object most fitting his proud behaviour—an Ass. Thereafter Rabadash the Peacemaker was known more popularly as Rabadash the Donkey! Lewis, *The Horse and His Boy*, 168–71.

70. Lewis, *Dawn Treader*, 86.

71. Nellas, *Deification in Christ*, 40. In relation to the painful process of transformation Lewis would most likely have preferred the term "mortification." See Lewis, *The Problem of Pain*, 406.

72. Lewis, *Dawn Treader*, 89.

and from all your idols. Moreover, I will give you a new heart and put a new spirit within you; and I will remove the heart of stone from your flesh and give you a heart of flesh." In reference to Ezekiel 36 John Calvin offers a complementary interpretation to the allusion as used by Lewis when he writes,

> On the other hand, it behooves us to consider the sort of remedy by which divine grace corrects and cures the corruption of nature. Since the Lord in coming to our aid bestows upon us what we lack, when the nature of his work in us appears, our destitution will, on the other hand, at once be manifest. When the apostle tells the Philippians he is confident "that he who began a good work in you will bring it to completion at the day of Jesus Christ" [Philippians 1:6], there is no doubt that through "the beginning of a good work" he denotes the very origin of conversion itself, which is in the will. God begins his good work in us, therefore, by arousing love and desire and zeal for righteousness in our hearts; or, to speak more correctly, by bending, forming, and directing, our hearts to righteousness. He completes his work, moreover, by confirming us to perseverance. In order that no one should make an excuse that good is initiated by the Lord to help the will which by itself is weak, the Spirit elsewhere declares what the will, left to itself, is capable of doing: "A new heart shall I give you, and will put a new spirit within you; and I will remove the heart of stone from your flesh, and give you a heart of flesh. And I shall put my spirit within you, and cause you to walk in my statutes" [Ezekiel 36:26–27]. Who shall say that the infirmity of the human will is strengthened by his help in order that it may aspire effectively to the choice of good, when it must rather be wholly transformed and renewed?
>
> If in a stone there is such plasticity that, made softer by some means, it becomes somewhat bent, I will not deny that man's heart can be molded to obey the right, provided what is imperfect in him be supplied by God's grace. But if by this comparison the Lord wished to show that nothing good can ever be wrung from our heart, unless it become wholly other, let us not divide between him and us what he claims for himself alone. If, therefore, a stone is transformed into flesh when God converts us to zeal for the right, whatever is of our own will is effaced. What takes its place is wholly from God.[73]

---

73. Calvin, *Institutes*, 2.3.6: "Men's inability to do good manifests itself above all in the work of redemption, which God does quite alone."

The motif of the pain involved in our transposition into the likeness of God is often emphasized by Lewis. In *The Problem of Pain*, one of Lewis's most famous lines appears in this context and explains the way that God uses human suffering and pain as an instrument in our transformation: "God whispers to us in our pleasures, speaks in our conscience, but shouts in our pain: it is His megaphone to rouse a deaf world."[74] With Eustace Scrubb's transformation firmly in mind, we may note how Lewis goes on to say:

> Now God, who has made us, knows what we are and that our happiness lies in Him. Yet we will not seek it in Him as long as He leaves us any other resort where it can even plausibly be looked for. While what we call "our own life" remains agreeable we will not surrender it to Him. What then can God do in our interests but make "our own life" less agreeable to us, and take away the plausible sources of false happiness?[75]

Devin Brown helpfully points out that Lewis provides a moving account of his own spiritual transformation to Arthur Greeves, one that mirrors that of Eustace Scrubb's attempt to remove his own layers of dragon skin. "In a letter dated January 30, 1930, Lewis writes about his battle with his "besetting sin" of pride and observes, "I have found out ludicrous and terrible things about my own character. . . . There seems to be no end to it. Depth under depth of self-love and self-admiration."[76] In *Mere Christianity*, when Lewis discusses the higher nature of faith, he describes the process of moral effort required in Christian transformation as a "road of moral effort, of trying harder and harder." However, he immediately goes on to add, "But in another sense it is not trying that is ever going to bring us home. All this trying leads up to the vital moment at which you turn to God and say, 'You must do this, I can't.'"[77]

---

74. Lewis, *The Problem of Pain*, 406.
75. Ibid., 408.
76. Brown, "Further Up and Further In."
77. Lewis, *Mere Christianity*, 115. Perhaps Lewis had in mind the sober teaching of Jesus in Matthew 7:14 that following Jesus involves walking along the "narrow way that leads to life, and there are few who find it." "Narrow" here is the perfect passive form of the verb *thlibō*; that is, narrow because this path squashes one on both sides with hardships and sorrows of all kinds. This merely echoes Jesus's words in Matthew 10.38, 39 that "He who does not take his cross and follow after me is not worthy of me. He who has found his life will lose it, and he who has lost his life for my sake will find it." Here we may think of the teaching of 2 Timothy 3:12 where Paul informs us that "indeed, all who

A similar imaginative scene is depicted in *The Great Divorce*, wherein a ghostly resident of Hell with a little red lizard (sexual lust) on his shoulder is confronted by a radiant Angel who offers to slay the lizard.[78] Only reluctantly does the Ghost give in to the Angel's relentless offers but when the Angel begins the Ghost is in fear of his life and winces from the pain of the process. To this the Angel replies, "I never said I wouldn't hurt you. I said it wouldn't kill you."[79] We also see a vivid picture in this story of the integral connection between the sovereignty of God and the freedom of the will. Eight times in this short exchange the Angel asks the Ghost if he may kill the lizard, explicitly asking "Have I your permission?"[80] Without such permission the Angel would not force his will upon the Ghost. We also see that the Ghost does not have it in him to slay the lizard himself: "I'm sure I shall be able to keep [the lizard] in order now. I think the gradual process would be far better than killing it," says the Ghost. To which the Angel replies, "The gradual process is no use at all."[81] Moral effort, heavenly grace, and transformation are what mark out Lewis's appropriation of theosis. After Eustace was a boy again he appeared to Edmund but he did not immediately recognise him.[82] Eustace initially appeared as a dark figure in the distance, too small to be Caspian, but too big to be Lucy. "Who are you?" asked Edmund; "Don't you know me? . . . It's me—Eustace."[83] And Eustace it was, the same little boy who had fallen into the picture at the beginning of the story, and yet a very different young man after his encounter with Aslan. So too the Ghost and the lizard, who, after the Angel killed the lizard both it and the Ghost were transformed; the Ghost into a majestic man just slightly smaller than an Angel, and the lizard the greatest stallion "silvery white but with a main and tail of gold."[84]

In his intellectual and aesthetic autobiography, *Surprised by Joy*, Lewis exchanges the dragon flesh of Eustace Scrubb for images of his own

desire to live godly in Jesus Christ will be persecuted."

78. Lewis, *The Great Divorce*, 89–96.
79. Ibid., 84.
80. Ibid.
81. Ibid., 83.
82. Perhaps here we have a direct allusion to Jesus's appearance to Mary at his resurrection, wherein she mistakes Jesus for the gardener until he reveals himself to her—the same Jesus that entered the tomb, and yet now a more glorious manifestation of himself in his resurrected body. John 20:11–18.
83. Lewis, *Dawn Treader*, 83.
84. Lewis, *The Great Divorce*, 93.

imprisonment to his self-will, that of "some stiff clothing, like corsets, or even a suit of armour, as if I were a lobster."[85] In the fictional account of Eustace Scrubb's transformation into a dragon and back into a boy we catch a glimpse of how Lewis understood the process of theosis, much like the process Jesus spoke of in reference to his own death, "Truly, truly, I say to you, unless a grain of wheat falls into the earth and dies, it remains alone; but if it dies, it bears much fruit" (John 12:24). Lewis makes it clear that for Eustace, for Lewis himself, and for all who would seek to be transformed into the image of God, the process is a long and painful "undulation" but the result is beautiful and glorious. As Screwtape advises Wormwood, God "cannot ravish. He can only woo. For His ignoble idea is to eat the cake and have it; the creatures are to be one with Him, and yet themselves."[86]

OF THIS AND OTHER WORLDS

With much of the Great Tradition, Lewis considers the ultimate end for the believer is to participate in the Divine nature. Consequently he was compelled to write on the reality of our life beyond this life in his works of fiction. Throughout Lewis's fiction there is the dominant theme of the transfiguration of matter and the human being, and the moral prerequisite leading up to it.[87] We see this, for instance, at the close of "Man or Rabbit?," where we read, "Morality is a mountain which we cannot climb by our own efforts; and if we could we should only perish in the ice and unbreathable air of the summit, lacking those wings with which the rest of the journey has to be accomplished. For it is from there that the real ascent begins. The ropes and axes are 'done away' and the rest is a matter of flying."[88]

As the world of Narnia draws to a close and the "real Narnia"—the new heavens and new earth of Lewis's fabled land—is entered into by the righteous inhabitants of old Narnia, Lewis closes his fantasy epic with these words which reiterate his doctrine of theosis:

---

85. Lewis, *Surprised by Joy*, 211.

86. Lewis, *The Screwtape Letters*, 23. I am indebted to Devin Brown, "Further Up and Further In" for this reference.

87. One thinks of such works of fiction as *The Chronicles of Narnia*, *The Screwtape Letters*, *The Great Divorce*, *The Pilgrim's Regress*, and *Till We Have Faces*.

88. Lewis, "Man or Rabbit?," 73.

"You do not yet look so happy as I mean you to be."

Lucy said, "We're so afraid of being sent away, Aslan. And you have sent us back into our own world so often."

"No fear of that," said Aslan. "Have you not guessed?"

Their hearts leaped and a wild hope rose within them.

"There was a real railway accident," said Aslan softly. "Your father and mother and all of you are—as you used to call it in the Shadowlands—dead. The term is over: the holidays have begun. The dream is ended: this is the morning."

And as he spoke he no longer looked to them like a lion; but things that began to happen after that were so great and beautiful that I cannot write them. And for us this is the end of all the stories, and we can most truly say that they all lived happily ever after. But for them it was only the beginning of the real story. All their life in this world and all their adventures in Narnia had only been the cover and the title page: now at last they were beginning Chapter One of the Great Story which no one on earth has read: which goes on forever: in which every chapter is better than the one before.[89]

Theosis appeals to me, I think, for some of the same reasons it appealed to Lewis. In one of her letters to Lewis, Evelyn Underhill summarized this appeal in a sentence when she wrote, "It is this capacity for giving imaginative body to the fundamental doctrines of Christianity that seems to me one of the most remarkable things about your work."[90] Theosis is one biblically and traditionally sanctioned vehicle for the expression of salvation in such imaginative terms. I conclude with one final image from the theological imagination of Lewis. On the lips of the noble unicorn Lewis places some of the finest words ever spoken in the lands of Narnia, and some of the most well-known: "I have come home at last! This is my real country! I belong here. This is the land I have been looking for all my life, though I never knew it till now. The reason why we loved the old Narnia is that it sometimes looked a little like this. Bree-hee-hee! Come further up, come further in!"[91]

---

89. Lewis, *The Last Battle*, 165.
90. Underhill, *Letters*, 301.
91. Ibid., 161.

8

A Narnian Way to Heaven

Judgment, Universalism, and Hell in Lewis's Vision

MARTIN SUTHERLAND

C. S. LEWIS HAD a vision of Hell as a state apparently chosen by the individual. Those who will not receive the grace of God bring on their own damnation. However, this unusual eschatology, though personal, is in fact not individualistic. This chapter argues that Lewis's vision hinges on his relational view of human personhood, where the interaction implied by speech and hearing are essential. Speech is creative and indicative, as is the ability to hear. In later works this relational concept focuses on the "Face"—a cypher for Lewis of relational personhood.

C. S. Lewis died on 22 November 1963. It happened that two other notable figures died that very day: the novelist Aldous Huxley and the American President, John F. Kennedy. This coincidence provided the pretext for philosopher Peter Kreeft's 1982 work, *Between Heaven and Hell*. In this work, employing a literary device favoured by philosophers over the centuries, Kreeft describes an imaginary conversation between Lewis as orthodox Christian, Huxley as pantheist and Kennedy as Western humanist. The title of the work, *Between Heaven and Hell*, suggests something of the notions behind it. Why the conversation at all? Because it gives an opportunity, a last chance for Huxley and Kennedy to accept the truth Lewis sets forth and to find themselves ultimately in heaven rather than hell. Kreeft adds a subtitle "a dialogue somewhere beyond death." Once again we are pointed to the key issues. What is this "somewhere between" and are we really to perceive it as a transient, rather than a permanent, state? In the dialogue, John F. Kennedy wrestles with this problem.

> Kennedy: . . .What do I mean by purgatory? I never thought much about it. But most Catholics believed it was a place where you had to go to suffer for your sins. What do you think?
> Lewis: I suspect that idea is not wholly wrong, but not wholly right either. I think it's more likely that purgatory is a place for education rather than suffering—a sort of "remedial reading" of your earthly life. As such it is really the first part of heaven, not a distinct place. So I think we are being prepared for deep heaven if this is purgatory.[1]

This notion of the second chance, an option to find redemption even after physical death, resonates with much in Lewis's work. However, Lewis's proposal is more that the processes of both redemption and damnation are already begun in life and continue after death. This in turn needs to be set and understood in the sophisticated personal eschatology which Lewis devised, only some aspects of which can be explored here. This chapter will focus on two key elements and one implication of Lewis's vision. Central to any understanding of Lewis's eschatology is, firstly, his perception of the nature of Judgment. The active agency of Judgment is human, rather than divine. Secondly, we must grasp his vision of the incommensurate natures of Heaven and Hell. They are not alternative realties or even states. The former is real, the latter unreal. Thus, for Lewis, Hell is delusion and Judgment an election for unreality. This schema has important implications. In particular it reveals that Lewis's picture of the afterlife of the person depends on his notions of personhood itself.

A CHOSEN DELUSION

The difference between Heaven and Hell is that of the difference between reality and delusion, between infinite richness and utter impoverishment, between endless discovery and bland impersonality. In a powerful set of literary metaphors and images which echo Dickens in *Bleak House* and Kafka in *The Trial and the Castle*, Lewis exposes hell in terms of faceless

1. Kreeft, *Between Heaven and Hell*, 21.

and dehumanizing bureaucracies. The narrative structure of *The Screwtape Letters*, for instance, situates its key protagonist in a superefficient (and therefore pitilessly functional and lifeless) office block—the "Infernal Lowerarchy." Lewis, the Romantic, had developed an aversion to the "world of 'Admin.'" In such a world reality may be kept at one remove; pain and consequences reduced to collateral damage. As Wayne Martindale explains, "like any bureaucracy, Hell chews up individuals in favour of the abstract collective." Ironically, however:

> The collective good, as it turns out, is a convenient excuse or philosophical cover for the selfishness and greed of those capable of seizing power.... "We must picture Hell," says Lewis, "as a state where everyone is perpetually concerned about his own dignity and advancement, where everyone has a grievance, and where everyone lives the deadly serious passions of envy, self-importance and resentment."[2]

The same concerns emerge in the Space Trilogy. In *Perelandra*, Weston's self-centered hubris, far from crowning and fulfilling his humanity, destroys it. In *That Hideous Strength* the "National Institute of Co-ordinated Experiments" (N.I.C.E.) is a disturbing expression of the destructive power of emotional and moral distance. A village may be destroyed for the greater good. Heads are disconnected from their troublesome bodies. In the "ideal" world even the need for sex would be eliminated. In such worlds reality is the challenge and the problem. Indeed, the real is cause for revulsion, to be eliminated in the cause of a false ideal.

These portrayals of evil reflect a deeper reality still: that hell is about delusion. *The Great Divorce* (1945) explores this in poignant detail. Lewis was intrigued by the peripheral Catholic notion of the Refrigerium or a "Holiday from Hell." The narrative structure of the book thus consists of a day excursion for the inhabitants "Grey Town," a place of shadows and chimera. In this "boring place peopled with bores"[3] the inhabitants are constantly quarrelling because of (not despite) the fact that it is a realm in which you get everything you wish for. Here you get only the illusions you yourself create.

Only the illusions you yourself create. If delusion, falseness and divorce from reality lie at the heart of Lewis's vision of hell, so choice is central to his understanding of Judgment, indeed to the entire structure of his

---

2. Martindale, *Beyond the Shadowlands*, 154–55.
3. Ibid., 180.

personal eschatology. Judgment is shifted from the notion of a wrathful God to the (surprising) preference of the creature. In Kreeft's imaginary conversation, John F. Kennedy asks, "Can you imagine a worse God than one who claps human beings into hell for all eternity?"

Lewis: Yes, I can imagine a much worse God than that.

Kennedy: What God?

Lewis: One who would put people in hell who didn't deserve it. An unjust God. But the God I believe in is not only above injustice, he's also above justice. He's pure love.

Kennedy: Wonderful! Then there is no hell.

Lewis: That does not follow.

Kennedy: Why not? How could pure love create hell?

Lewis: I don't think God creates hell; I think we do, or perhaps evil spirits do.

Kennedy: But God puts you there.

Lewis: No again, we put ourselves there by free choice.[4]

For Lewis, Judgment and Damnation—Hell itself—are created for themselves by those who reject the only true reality, that created by God. Partway through the excursion in The Great Divorce, the narrator meets one of the "solid people"—someone from the real place, Heaven—who turns out to be one of Lewis's favourite authors, George MacDonald. MacDonald instructs him on this hell of our own choosing.

The narrator asks, "Are Heaven and Hell only states of mind?" "Hush," his teacher sternly responds. "Do not blaspheme. Hell is a state of mind. . . . But Heaven is not a state of mind. Heaven is reality itself."[5] So, Heaven and Hell are not alternative realities. One is real, the other is unreal. For Lewis the Damned cling to their own preferred vision of what is "real." "The theme that runs through each of the meetings between the Solid People of Heaven and the Ghosts of Hell is choice . . . sin is ultimately the choosing of self over God. Damnation and Hell are receiving that choice of self over God forever."[6] It is a vision ultimately unmasked as folly, but is clung to

---

4. Kreeft, *Between Heaven and Hell*, 18–19.
5. Lewis, *The Great Divorce*, 63.
6. Martindale, *Beyond the Shadowlands*, 183.

out of pride. "There are only two kinds of people in the end:" MacDonald reveals, "those who say to God, "Thy will be done" and those to whom God says, in the end, "Thy will be done."⁷

In chapter 13 of *The Last Battle* Lewis draws a truly memorable picture of this self-chosen delusion. It is a scene eerily paralleling Kreeft's "dialog." After a sudden transition from the tumult of battle, Tirian finds himself in a wide and beautiful place. Also present there are seven Kings and Queens of Narnia (Susan alone is missing). It is a place "somewhere beyond death," but not everyone can see its wideness or its beauty. A company of dwarves remains convinced they are held in a dark and foul stable. Distrustful in the extreme, they suspect all notions of reality offered by others. Nothing which can be said or done will convince them otherwise. Even the arrival of Aslan brings no enlightenment. "'You see,' said Aslan, 'they will not let us help them. They have chosen cunning instead of belief. Their prison is only in their own minds, yet they are in that prison; and so afraid of being taken in that they cannot be taken out.'"⁸

Thus, for Lewis, Hell is not a matter of God imposing a punishment. It is, rather, his act of love in allowing the creature the (perverted) exercise of their freedom.

We damn ourselves.

Matthew Lee shows that this is Lewis's solution to the logical difficulty at the heart of the classic doctrine of Hell. Lee suggests the problem emerges from the essential incoherency of holding together four key premises.

1. If anyone is perfectly good, then that person does not torment anyone . . . eternally.
2. If anyone is in hell then God torments that person . . . eternally.
3. God is perfectly good.
4. There are some people who are in hell. ⁹

Solutions are available to this apparent incoherency but they come from challenging one or more of the premises. (A universalist might challenge premise four, a process theologian might nuance "perfection" in premise three, a philosopher might question the nature of "good" in premises one and three, etc.) Lewis's solution is to rethink premise two. As Lee points out, "It is not that Lewis rejects the traditional notion that Hell is a

---

7. Lewis, *The Great Divorce*, 66–67.
8. Lewis, *The Last Battle*, 135.
9. Lee, "To Reign in Hell or to Serve in Heaven," 160.

place of eternal torment. What Lewis denies is that God is the tormenter, either remotely or immediately."[10] It is as with the dwarves in *The Last Battle*.

> The denizens of hell are their own tormentors. They psychotically cling to their addictions, to the wrongs they have suffered, to petty lusts and to their "rights." They will not forgive, will not admit wrongdoing, and will not be ruled; they make themselves miserable, but will not believe that a better way is open to them.[11]

Lee rightly intuits that there are profound implications for personhood in Lewis's eschatology. It is my contention, however, that Lee does not take the questions far enough. Starting, not unreasonably, with Lewis's vision of Heaven as the more potent category, Lee comes to describe Lewis's Hell in terms of free will. In order to become those who enjoy God, humans must be creatures of free will. There is, however, an intrinsic shadow side to free will: namely, the capacity to turn away. "Hell, then, is simply the culmination of a pattern of free choice to turn away from God and to be on one's own."[12] So far so good—we have already seen that choice is essential to the self-created delusion of Hell. Not just any choice, but choice for the self.

Writing on "Two Ways with the Self" in *The Guardian* on 3 May 1940, Lewis was quite clear on the pernicious evil of preference for self.

> Now, the self can be regarded in two ways. On the one hand, it is God's creature, an occasion of love and rejoicing; now, indeed, hateful in condition but to be pitied and healed. On the other hand, it is that one self of all others which is called I and me, and which on that ground puts forward an irrational claim to preference. This claim is to be not only hated, but simply killed; "never," as George MacDonald says, "to be allowed a moment's respite from eternal death." [13]

This drives a wider notion of externality—of seeking the "other"—which connects us in turn to longing, and hence to Lewis's key notion of "Joy." As Judith Wolfe has recently pointed out, "Lewis consistently valorizes knowledge and enjoyment of things outer and other than the self over

---

10 Ibid., 161.
11 Ibid., 166.
12. Ibid.
13. Lewis, "Two Ways with the Self," 154–56.

self-reflection: humans are most alive and authentic when absorbed in their interests, friends or pursuits."[14]

In *The Problem of Pain* Lewis addresses directly the problem of Judgment. Is it God who condemns? Lewis's answer is clearly "no"—"we are to think of this bad man's perdition not as a sentence imposed on him but as the mere fact of being what he is."

> The characteristic of lost souls "is their rejection of everything that is not simply themselves." Our imaginary egoist has tried to turn everything he meets into a province or appendage of the self. The taste for the other, that is, the very capacity for enjoying good, quenched in him except in so far as his body still draws him into some rudimentary contact with an outer world. Death removes this last contact. He has had his wish—to lie wholly in the self and to make the best of what he finds there. And what he find there is Hell.[15]

It is this choice for the self over the ultimate "Other"—God—which self-damns the lost. This is as far as Lee's argument takes the question of personhood in relation to this Hell of self-choice. That Lee feels no need to explore further is unsurprising, given that his key enquiry is, as the title of his paper indicates, "the problem of hell and the enjoyment of the good." In the present chapter, however, the principle interest is in Lewis's connections between Heaven, Hell and personhood, rather than the Good. So we must push further.

A RELATIONAL PERSONHOOD

Free will does not of itself supply a sufficient understanding of the view of personhood which lies at the heart of Lewis's eschatology. Humans are blessed/cursed with free will to be sure, but this is merely as aspect of the deeper reality that they are creatures uniquely capable of transforming relationships with the divine.

In *The Last Battle*, a few pages on from the description of the state of the Dwarves, is the depiction of a more general judgment, akin to a cosmic, rather than a merely personal event.

---

14. Wolfe, "C. S. Lewis and the Eschatological Church," 114.

15. Lewis, *The Problem of Pain*, 418. The quotation Lewis uses is from von Hugel, *Essays and Addresses*, first series, "What Do We Mean by Heaven and Hell?"

> The creatures came rushing on, their eyes brighter and brighter as they drew nearer and nearer to the standing Stars. But as they came right up to Aslan, one or other of two things happened to each of them. They all looked straight in his face; I don't think they had any choice about that. And when some looked, the expression of their faces changed terribly—it was all fear and hatred: except that, on the faces of the Talking Beasts, the fear and hatred lasted only a fraction of a second. You could see that they suddenly ceased to be Talking Beasts. They were just ordinary animals. And all the creatures who looked at Aslan in that way swerved to their right, his left, and disappeared into his huge black shadow.[16]

In this dramatic picture we see again the elements already identified in Lewis's eschatology. Most obvious are the exercise and the result of individual choice. David Downing describes it like this:

> [I]n Lewis's understanding, this moment of reckoning is not so much a day of Judgment as a Day of Acknowledgement.
> As all the talking creatures of that world come face to face with Aslan, they turn one way, to bliss and fellowship, or they turn another, into the shadow. . . . But the path they take, towards light or shadow, is not determined by Aslan's face as he looks at them. Rather it is determined by their faces as they look at him.[17]

I will argue that Downing's interpretation places too much on the "faces" of the creatures and needs to be nuanced by Lewis's view of "glory." The importance of choice is certainly clear, but there is more to be read from this scene. In addition to choice, there is a hint of a fundamental capacity, something which lies at the heart of the opportunity to be saved and, moreover, the nature of that salvation. The fate of some of the talking beasts is the interesting one—"they suddenly ceased to be Talking Beasts. They were just ordinary animals."

Stephen Webb has argued for the importance of the voice in the Narnian stories.

> Lewis defends a vocative philosophy of sound. What does that mean? In brief, a vocative philosophy of sound argues that the meaning of words is most fundamentally found in the human voice. . . . In our culture today, it is tempting to think that meaning has to do with the silent and abstract properties of sentences.

---

16. Lewis, *The Last Battle*, 138–40.
17. Downing, *Into the Wardrobe*, 82.

> Truth is something we see on the written page. Lewis helps us understand that meaning is sonic before it is visual.

Voices, however, are fragile. We can literally lose our voices due to stress or sickness. We can also be afraid to speak for a variety of reasons. To be given a voice, then is to be set free. Likewise, to be denied a voice is to be denied one's humanity.[18]

In *The Magician's Nephew*, Jadis, Queen of Charn (later the White Witch), exterminates everyone in Charn by uttering the Deplorable Word. The foolish, evil Uncle Andrew is confirmed as such by the fact that he cannot hear the created beasts' noise as language. Conversely, Narnia is called into being by the voice of Aslan and his speech and voice are determinative again at its end, in *The Last Battle*.

Speech, the ability to communicate, is what makes the creatures "persons." More than that, it is the point at which they image Aslan. All through the Narnia books Aslan's voice is what determines outcomes and responses. Those who speak bear the stamp of that quality. At the moment of judgment (or, if you prefer, "acknowledgement"), when their choices regarding Aslan are revealed, they either enter through the door, or are swept away, persons no more. "They suddenly ceased to be Talking Beasts. They were just ordinary animals." This distinction between talking and non-talking is essential and deliberate. In Narnia, that which makes us able to respond to the saving relationship with Aslan—to be persons, to be "real" in the heavenly sense—is the ability to speak, to communicate meaning in words. Those who enter Aslan's country are speechifiers.

To identify the point to the loss of speech in the Narnian judgment with a loss of rationality is too reductionist. It is better, I suggest, to see it as the loss of relationality. But just as those who enter that country are called upon to go "farther up and farther in" so we must explore what it is to be "person" in Lewis's vision. Speech or voice is not of itself the deep reality of the person. Voice can be insincere; speech can decay into gibberish. This is a flaw Lewis acknowledges in his poem "Legion," published in 1955.[19]

---

18. Webb, "Aslan's Voice," 7.
19. Lewis, "Legion."

A NARNIAN WAY TO HEAVEN

FACES

Voice may be crucial to personhood but its mere presence is no passport to reality. That essential reality is explored in Lewis's challenging last novel, *Till We Have Faces*. Much of the complexity of this novel in fact derives from the literary "voice" that is used. All of Lewis's fiction to that date had been written in third person, "eye of God," format, with the assumed bonus that this narrator is reliable and honest. *Till We Have Faces* is a retelling of the myth of Psyche. In Lewis's work, however the story is told from the point of view of Orual, Psyche's possessive sister. Indeed it is a narrative of self-justification. The story is thus much more profoundly about Orual than it is about Psyche. Crucially, Orual wears a veil for most of the story, hiding her face.

Not surprisingly, given the title of the book, the "face," in this case the veiled face, is crucial to the themes of the story. What are we to make of it? Doris Myers sees Orual's journey, climaxing in the unveiling and the unloading of her complaint against the gods as a passage towards Jungian individuation. "By reading aloud the inner version of her book . . . Orual has come to know that her confrontation is with herself. In the beginning, she taunted the gods for refusing to answer her complaint; at the end she learned that her answer came from herself."[20]

This seems unlikely, and out of step with Lewis's consistent motif of outwardness as a higher path than self-absorption. We should look for something more than a psychological model of the self. Clyde Kilby, identifying the "face" motif as significant also in *That Hideous Strength*, recognises Lewis's call to embrace the real. "Very much is said in this story about faces, the most significant being the veiled face, actual and symbolical, of Orual. By having a face Lewis means a willingness to be honest with the truths of the whole universe, not some selected ones that suit one's prejudices or a given climate of opinion."[21]

However, something more profound even than clear-sightedness is at stake. Orual's face is symbolic of her humanity, of her personality, of her capacity for salvific relationship. As Charles Huttar (following Peter Schakel) puts it, Orual's veil

> allows her to bury her personal self and establishes a barrier between herself and others, and herself and the divine. She has no

---

20. Myers, *Bareface*, 132. See also 199–203.
21. Kilby, *Images of Salvation*, 137–38.

face, no identity, and thus has no way to relate to the divine. Only when she removes the veil, confronts her true self, and gains a "face" can she encounter God face-to-face, without defences, excuses or pretence. Only then can she attain an authentic relationship with God, with others and with herself. [22]

As she comes to full realization Orual understands her own development.

> When the time comes to you at which you will be forced at last to utter the speech which has lain at the centre of your soul for years, which you have, all that time, idiot-like, been saying over and over, you'll not talk about joy of words. I saw well why the gods do not speak to us openly, nor let us answer. Till that word can be dug out of us, why should they hear the babble that we think we mean? How can they meet us face to face till we have faces?[23]

At Orual's moment of revelation even words, as important as they are in Lewis's world, drop away. We see in this a resolution similar to that in Job 42:1–6. There too had been a quest of complaint, with incomplete versions of reality presented to the protagonist, who remained dissatisfied until an encounter with the divine. Crucially the resolution is not in the form of direct answer to either Job or Orual. Job, for instance, does not get the explanation of his suffering which he had been seeking. Instead he meets God. "I had heard of you by the hearing of the ear, but now my eye sees you" (Job 42:5).

Orual similarly writes: "I ended my first book with the words No Answer. I know now, Lord, why you utter no answer. You are yourself the answer. Before your face questions die away. What other answer would suffice?"[24]

As we have seen, Heaven for Lewis is the truly Real, whereas Hell is self-created illusion. We also see that only those who are themselves most real may enter this Heaven. This personal reality—signified in voice or face—is not some inner essence, but a function of relationship. A veiled Orual, "has no face, no identity, and thus has no way to relate to the divine." Only when she removes the veil, confronts her true self, and gains a "face"

---

22. Huttar, "Till We Have Faces," 403–5. Huttar is clearly dependent on Schakel's earlier work. The quotation appears almost unchanged in Schakel's "Till We Have Faces," 287.

23. Lewis, *Till We Have Faces*, 305.

24. Ibid., 319.

can she encounter God face-to-face, without defences, excuses or pretence. Only then can she attain an authentic relationship with God, with others and with herself.

In this we find a crucial link to Lewis's most famous sermon, "The Weight of Glory" (1941). Lee, in his exploration of Lewis's hell and the Good, also makes this link, though (as I will argue) unsatisfactorily. In this sermon, Lewis expands on the promised "glory" of the saved, first in the analogy of fame with God—approval—and then, secondarily, in the sense of luminescence or shining. A modern false modesty should not he argues, discourage us from aspiring to God's approbation. In the central point of his argument Lewis employs the same symbol that describes Orual's redemption. "In the end, that Face which is the delight or the terror of the universe must be turned upon each of us either with one expression or with the other, either conferring glory inexpressible or inflicting shame that can never be cured or disguised."[25]

But "glory" is a far richer experience than mere juridical verification. It is nothing less than the consummation of the divine-human relationship, found in union with Christ, the moment of ultimate gift, of personhood. "We shall be true and everlasting and really divine persons only in heaven."[26] "For glory meant good report with God, acceptance by God, response, acknowledgement, and welcome into the heart of things."[27] Glory is a way of describing salvation itself.

It is here that I find a necessary point of departure from Lee's treatment. Lee contends that "Lewis's vision of heaven derives from the beatific-vision tradition," that view which finds salvation most completely in knowing God as He truly is (see, e.g., 1 John 3:2). As will be seen, I will suggest this is a misinterpretation. Even if this fundamental point were to be accepted, however, Lee juxtaposes the concepts strangely. He distinguishes between Lewis's version of the beatific vision and his notion of glory. Glory is reduced to transformation—the transformation required in advance if the vision of God is truly to be a blessed one. Thus, in Lee's analysis, "the attainment of glory is a necessary condition for the beatific vision." Glory becomes, at least logically, prior to beatific vision.

This is at once to diminish Lewis's category of "glory" and to overanalyse his treatment of the vision of God. Glory is an outcome, not the

25. Lewis, "The Weight of Glory," 96.
26. Lewis, "Membership," 43.
27. Lewis, "The Weight of Glory," 98.

process. Moreover the two are described by Lewis, in passages quoted by Lee, in terms so resonant with each other as to preclude distinction. In his introduction to *The Four Loves*, Lewis defends the value and status of "need-love" in an argument which almost exactly parallels that of his treatment of desire for reward in "The Weight of Glory." He then suggests that the states in which a man is "nearest to God are those in which he is most surely and swiftly approaching his *final union with God, vision of God and enjoyment of God*" (emphasis added).[28]

The emphasised phrases are those cited by Lee to establish Lewis's connection to the beatific vision tradition.[29] But when we return to the earlier sermon, "The Weight of Glory," we see the same arguments employed to support a vision of salvation as "glory." "For glory meant good report with God, acceptance by God, response, acknowledgement, and welcome into the heart of things."[30] Lewis is merely describing (in different ways, nearly twenty years apart) the same blessed state. Lee's analysis errs in distinguishing between the two, and plainly misreads Lewis in suggesting a logical priority to glory. It might in fact be more in keeping with Lewis's picture to do the opposite, to recognise that glory is the blessed outcome for the saved of meeting the gaze of God. "The promise of glory is the promise, almost incredible and only possible by the work of Christ, that some of us, that any of us who really chooses, shall actually survive that examination, shall find approval, shall please God."[31] However, such a reversal would be to repeat the same error, to reduce one category to a process and to over-analyse the other. We are much better to see both glory and vision as aspects of the one outcome.

This is because the essence of Lewis's version of the beatific vision (if it can be called that at all) is not the creature's view of the creator (as in accordance with the tradition and in Lee's analysis), but rather the moment of standing in the creator's vision. When, in "The Weight of Glory," Lewis describes the hope of heaven as "attaining everlasting life in the vision of God,"[32] it is clear that the saving vision is God's, not the Christian's. "Indeed, how we think of Him is of no importance except in so far as it is related to

---

28. Lewis, *The Four Loves*, 13.
29. Lee, "To Reign in Hell or to Serve in Heaven," 162.
30. Lewis, "The Weight of Glory," 98.
31. Ibid., 96–97.
32. Ibid., 89.

A NARNIAN WAY TO HEAVEN

how He thinks of us. It is written that we shall "stand before" Him, shall appear, shall be inspected."[33]

Understanding this vision gives us clarity about judgment and salvation in Lewis. They are not equivalent, though opposite, events. One is real, the other unreal. Heaven is a place; Hell is a delusion. By choosing for ourselves we are opting for judgment, electing to enter Grey Town, a non-place, a Hell of our own fabulating. Salvation, by contrast, is not the mere product of self-contained choices by autonomous individuals. It is participation, through Christ, in the Trinitarian Divine life. This is the note on which Lewis concludes *Mere Christianity*.

> I am not, in my natural state, nearly so much of a person as I like to believe: most of what I call "me" can be very easily explained. It is when I turn to Christ, when I give myself up to His personality, that I first begin to have a real personality of my own.
>
> At the beginning I said there were personalities in God. I will go further now. There are no real personalities anywhere else. Until you have given up yourself to Him you will not have a real self.[34]

This is salvation. Crucially, it entails voice and engagement, it requires faces. It is found in meeting, indwelling and the perfection of love. At the moment of glory, the divine Person consummates the personhood of the creature. "We shall be true and everlasting and really divine persons only in heaven."[35] It is only this Heaven which is real. There is no true personhood, no salvation, other than in divinely bestowed glory.

---

33. Ibid., 96.
34. Lewis, *Mere Christianity*, 176–77.
35. Lewis, "Membership," 43.

Bibliography

WORKS BY C. S. LEWIS

The Abolition of Man. 1943. Repr., London: Collins, Fount, 1978.
The Collected Letters of C. S. Lewis. 3 vols. Edited by Walter Hooper. New York: Harper Collins, 2004–2007.
The Discarded Image: An Introduction to Medieval and Renaissance Literature. Cambridge: Cambridge University Press, 1967.
English Literature in the Sixteenth Century: Excluding Drama. Oxford: Oxford University Press, 1954.
Fern-Seed and Elephants: And Other Essays on Christianity. London: HarperCollins, 1975.
"The Funeral of a Great Myth." In *Christian Reflections*, edited by Walter Hooper, 110–23. London: Fount, 1981.
The Four Loves. London: Geoffrey Bles, 1960.
The Great Divorce. London: Geoffrey Bles, 1945.
A Grief Observed. London: Faber and Faber, 1966.
The Horse and His Boy. London: HarperCollins, 1954.
Introduction to *Athanasius on the Incarnation*. Translated and edited by a Religious of C.S.M.V. Crestwood, NY: St Vladimir's Orthodox Theological Seminary, 1989.
The Last Battle. Harmondsworth: Penguin, 1964.
"Man or Rabbit?" In *God in the Dock: Essays on Theology*, edited by Walter Hooper, 72. London: Fount, 1971.
"Meditation in a Toolshed." In *Compelling Reason: Essays on Ethics and Theology*, edited by Walter Hooper, 52–55. London: Fount, 1998.
"Membership." In *Transposition and Other Addresses,* 34–44. London: Geoffrey Bles, 1949.
Mere Christianity. London.: Geoffrey Bles, 1952.
Miracles. London: Geoffrey Bles, 1947.
Miracles. Rev. ed. London: Collins, Fontana, 1960.
The Pilgrim's Regress. London: HarperCollins, 1999.
Letters to Malcolm, Chiefly on Prayer. London: Geoffrey Bles, 1964.
"The Poison of Subjectivism." In *Christian Reflections.* London: Fount, 1981.
The Problem of Pain. In *The Complete C. S. Lewis Signature Classics*, 364–433. New York: HarperOne, 2002.
Reflections on the Psalms. 1940. Repr., London: Fontana, 1986.
The Screwtape Letters. New York: Bantam, 1982.
The Screwtape Letters, with Screwtape Proposes a Toast. New York: Macmillan, 1974.

BIBLIOGRAPHY

Surprised by Joy. London: Geoffrey Bles, 1955.
That Hideous Strength. New York: Scribner, 1996.
Till We Have Faces: A Myth Retold. London: William Collins, 1979.
"Transposition." In *Screwtape Proposes a Toast and Other Pieces*, 67–85. London: Fount, 1998.
"Version Vernacular." *The Christian Century* 75, December 1958, 515.
The Voyage of the Dawn Treader. London: HarperCollins, 1955.
"The Weight of Glory." In *Screwtape Proposes a Toast and Other Pieces*, 87–102. London: Fount, 1998.
"Vivisection." No pages. Online: http://www.irishantivivisection.org/cslewis.html.

OTHER WORKS CITED

Adams, Robert. "A Modified Divine Command Theory of Ethical Wrongness." In *Divine Commands and Morality*, 318–47. New York: Oxford University Press, 1981.
———. "Divine Command Meta-Ethics Modified Again." *Journal of Religious Ethics* 7/1 (1979): 66–79.
———. *Finite and Infinite Goods.* New York: Oxford University Press, 1999.
———. "Moral Arguments for Theistic Belief." in *The Virtue of Faith and Other Essays in Philosophical Theology*, edited by Robert Adams, 144–63. New York: Oxford University Press, 1987.
———. "Prospects for a Meta-ethical argument for Theism: A Response to Stephen Sullivan." *Journal of Religious Ethics* 21 (1993): 313–18.
Allchin, Arthur M. *Participation in God: A Forgotten Strand in Anglican Tradition.* Wilton, CT: Morehouse-Barlow, 1988.
Alston, William. "Some Suggestions for Divine Command Theorists." In *Christian Theism and the Problems of Philosophy*, edited by Michael Beaty, 303–4. Notre Dame, IN: University of Notre Dame Press, 1990.
Anderson, Clifford B. "A Pragmatic Reading of Karl Barth's Theological Epistemology." *American Journal of Theology & Philosophy* 22/3 (Sep 2001): 241.
Anscombe, G. E. M. *Metaphysics and the Philosophy of Mind: Collected Philosophical Papers, Volume II.* Oxford: Basil Blackwell, 1981.
Aquinas, Thomas. *Summa Theologica.* Chicago: William Benton, 1952.
Aristotle. *Generation of Animals.* Translated by A. L. Peck. Loeb Classical Library. Cambridge, MA: Harvard University Press, 1942.
Augustine. *City of God.* Chicago: William Benton, 1952.
———. *Confessions.* Chicago: William Benton, 1952.
Ball, Philip. *Shapes, Nature's Patterns: A Tapestry in Three Parts.* Oxford: Oxford University Press, 2009.
Barth, Karl. *Church Dogmatics* . Edited by G. W. Bromiley and T. F. Torrance. London: T&T Clark, 2004.
———. *The Word of God and the Word of Man.* Gloucester, MA: Peter Smith, 1957.
———. *Evangelical Theology.* Grand Rapids: Eerdmans, 1963.
———. *The Humanity of God.* Translated by James McNab. Edinburgh: Oliver and Boyd, 1959.
———. *How I Changed My Mind.* Edinburgh: The St. Andrews Press, 1966.

Beilby, James. *Naturalism Defeated? Essays on Platinga's Evolutionary Argument against Naturalism*. Ithaca, NY: Cornell University Press, 2002.

Bekoff, Marc. *The Animal Manifesto: Six Reasons for Expanding Our Compassion Footprint*. Novato, CA: New World Library, 2010.

Bekoff, Marc, and Jessica Pierce. *Wild Justice: The Moral Lives of Animals*. Chicago: University of Chicago Press, 2010.

Beversluis, John. *C. S. Lewis and the Search for Rational Religion*. Grand Rapids: Eerdmans, 1985.

Bouteneff, Peter. Foreword to Norman Russell, *Fellow Workers with God: Orthodox Thinking on Theosis*. Crestwood, NY: St Vladimir's Theological Seminary Press, 2009.

Bowron, Hugh. "Eastern Promises: Remedying the Pneumatological Deficits of Western Theology." In *The Spirit of Truth: Reading Scripture and Constructing Theology with the Holy Spirit*, edited by Myk Habets, 107–23. Eugene, OR: Pickwick Publications, 2010.

Braaten, Carl E., and Robert W. Jenson. *Union with Christ: The New Finnish Interpretation of Luther*. Grand Rapids: Eerdmans, 1998.

Bramlett, Perry C. "Transposition." In *The C. S. Lewis Readers' Encyclopedia*, 408–9. Grand Rapids: Zondervan, 1998.

Brink, David O. "The Autonomy of Ethics." In *The Cambridge Companion to Atheism*, edited by Michael Martin, 149–65. Cambridge: Cambridge University Press, 2007.

Broad, Charles D. "Berkeley's Theory of Morals." *Revue Internationale de Philosophie* 23/24 (1953): 72–86.

Brock, Stephen. "On Whether Aquinas's *Ipsum Esse* is 'Platonism.'" *The Review of Metaphysics* 60/2 (2006): 269.

Bromiley, Geoffrey W. *An Introduction to the Theology of Karl Barth*. Edinburgh: T&T Clark, 1979.

Brown, Devin. "'Further Up and Further In': Narnia as an Introduction to Lewis's Thought and Theology." Online: http://www.narniafaith.com/teach/study-guides-and-youth-resources/further-up-and-further-in-five-lessons-from-c-s-lewis-lesson-4/.

Bryne, Peter. "Moral Arguments for the Existence of God." *Stanford Encyclopedia of Philosophy*. Available at http://plato.stanford.edu/entries/moral-arguments-god/.

Busch, Eberhard. *Karl Barth*. Translated by J. Bowden. London: SCM Press, 1971.

———. *Karl Barth: His Life from Letters and Autobiographical Texts*. London: SCM Press, 1976.

Calvin, John. *The Institutes of the Christian Religion*. Edited by John T. McNeill. Translated by Ford L. Battles. Philadelphia: Westminster Press, 1960.

Card, Orson Scott. *Xenocide*. New York: Tor Books, 1991.

Carey, Nessa. *The Epigenetics Revolution*. London: Icon Books, 2011.

Carson, Thomas. *Value and the Good Life*. Notre Dame, IN: University of Notre Dame Press, 2000.

Choufrine, Arkadi. *Gnosis, Theophany, Theosis: Studies in Clement of Alexandria's Appropriation of His Background*. New York: Peter Lang, 2002.

Clendenin, Daniel B. *Eastern Orthodox Christianity: A Western Perspective*. Grand Rapids: Baker, 1994.

Conway Morris, Simon, ed. *The Deep Structure of Convergence: Is Convergence Sufficiently Ubiquitous to Give a Directional Signal?* West Conshohocken, PA: Templeton Foundation, 2009.

BIBLIOGRAPHY

———. *Life's Purpose: Inevitable Humans in a Lonely Universe*. Cambridge: Cambridge University Press, 2005.

Craig, William Lane. *Philosophical Foundations of a Christian World View*. Downers Grove, IL: InterVarsity Press, 2003.

———. "This Most Gruesome of Guests." In *Is Goodness without God Good Enough? A Debate on Faith, Secularism and Ethics*, edited by Robert K Garcia and Nathan L King, 167–88. Lantham, MD: Rowan and Littlefield Publishers, 2009.

Cross, R. "Perichoresis, Deification, and Christological Predication in John of Damascus." *Mediaeval Studies* 62 (2000): 69–124.

Churchland, Patricia. *Brain-Wise: Studies in Neurophilosophy*. Cambridge, MA: The MIT Press, 2002.

Darwall, Stephen. "Berkeley's Moral and Political Philosophy." In *The Cambridge Companion to Berkeley*, edited by Kenneth P. Winkler, 311–38. Cambridge: Cambridge University Press, 2005.

Derrick, Christopher. *C. S. Lewis and the Church of Rome: A Study in Proto-Ecumenism*. San Francisco: Ignatius Press, 1981.

Donnellan, Keith. "Reference and Definite Descriptions." *Philosophical Review* 75 (1966): 281–304.

Dorsett, Lyle W. *Seeking the Secret Place: The Spiritual Formation of C. S. Lewis*. Grand Rapids: Brazos Press, 2004.

Downie, R. S. "Cambridge Platonists" in *The Oxford Companion to Philosophy*, Ted Honderich (ed.), OUP, NY, 1995.

Downing, David C. *Into the Wardrobe: C. S. Lewis and the Narnia Chronicles*. San Francisco: Jossey-Bass, 2005.

Drever, Matthew. "The Self before God? Rethinking Augustine's Trinitarian Thought." *Harvard Theological Review* 100/2 (Apr 2007): 233.

Esselstyn, Calwell B. Jr. *Prevent and Reverse Heart Disease*. New York: Penguin, 2008.

Farrer, Austen. *The Brink of Mystery*. London: SPCK, 1976.

Filmer-Davies, C. "Gods, Heroes and Kings: The Battle for Mythic Britain." *Literature & Theology* 17/1 (Mar 2003): 100.

Finlan, Stephen. "Second Peter's Notion of Divine Participation," in *Theōsis: Deification in Christian Theology*, edited by Stephen Finlan and Vladimir Kharlamov, 32–50. Eugene, OR: Wipf & Stock, 2006.

Garcia, Robert K., and Nathan L. King, eds. *Is Goodness without God Good Enough?: A Debate on Faith, Secularism and Ethics*. Lanham, MD: Rowan & Littlefield Publishers, 2008.

Glazov, Gregory. "Theosis, Judaism, and Old Testament Anthropology," in *Theōsis: Deification in Christian Theology*, edited by Stephen Finlan and Vladimir Kharlamov, 16–31. Eugene, OR: Wipf & Stock, 2006.

Gollwitzer, Helmut. *Karl Barth's Church Dogmatics: Selections*. Edinburgh: T&T Clark, 1961.

Gotz, Ignacio. "On Inspiration." *Cross Currents* 48/4 (Winter 1998/1999): 510.

Gresham, Douglas H. *Lenten Lands*. London: Collins. 1990.

Griffin, William. *C. S. Lewis: The Authentic Voice*. New York: Harper & Row, 1986.

———. "What Is Mere Christianity?" At http://www.explorefaith.com.

Habets, M. *Theosis in the Theology of Thomas Torrance*. Surrey: Ashgate, 2009.

———. "'Reformed Theosis?' A Response to Gannon Murphy." *Theology Today* 65 (2009): 489–98.

———. "Theosis, Yes; Deification, No." In *The Spirit of Truth: Reading Scripture and Constructing Theology with the Holy Spirit*, edited by Myk Habets, 124–49. Eugene, OR: Pickwick Publications, 2010.

Hare, John. *God's Call: Moral Realism, God's Commands and Human Autonomy*. Grand Rapids: Eerdmans, 2001.

Hart, Trevor. *Regarding Karl Barth*. Cumbria, UK: Paternoster Press, 1999.

Haught, John. "Evolution and the Suffering of Sentient Life after Darwin." In *The Evolution of Evil*, edited by G. Bennett et al., 189–203. Göttingen: Vandenhoeck & Ruprecht, 2008.

Hay, David. *God's Biologist: A Life of Alister Hardy*. London: Darton, Longman & Todd, 2011.

Heraclitus. "Fragments." In *The Art and Thought of Heraclitus*, translated by Charles H. Kahn. Cambridge: Cambridge University Press, 1979.

Hoggard Creegan, Nicola. *Animal Suffering and the Problem of Evil*. Oxford: Oxford University Press, 2013.

Holmer, Paul L. *C. S. Lewis: The Shape of His Faith and Thought*. New York: Harper and Row, 1976.

Hooper, Walter. "Oxford's Bonny Fighter." In *C. S. Lewis at the Breakfast* Table, edited by James T. Como, 137–85. New York: Macmillan, 1979.

Hooper, Walter. Preface to *C. S. Lewis: Christian Reflections*, edited by Walter, vii–xiv. Grand Rapids: Eerdmans, 1967.

Huttar, Charles A. "Till We Have Faces." In *The C. S. Lewis Readers' Encyclopedia*, edited by Jeffrey.D. Schultz and John.G. West Jr., 403–5. Grand Rapids: Zondervan, 1998.

Hume, David A. *Treatise of Human Nature*. Edited by L. A. Selby-Bigge. Oxford: Clarendon Press, 1978.

Idziak, Janine Maree. "In Search of Good Positive Reasons for an Ethics of Divine Commands: A Catalogue of Arguments." *Faith and Philosophy* 6/1 (1989): 47–64.

Jensen, Chris. "Shine like the Son: C. S. Lewis and the Doctrine of Deification." *In Pursuit of Truth: A Journal of Christian Scholarship*. Online: http://www.cslewis.org/journal/author/chris-jensen/.

Kauffmann, Stuart. *Investigations*. Oxford: Oxford University Press, 2005.

Keating, Daniel A. *Deification and Grace*. Introductions to Catholic Theology. Washington, DC: Sapientia Press, 2007.

Kilby, Clyde S. *The Christian World of C. S. Lewis*. Grand Rapids: Eerdmans, 1964.

———. *Images of Salvation in the Fiction of C. S. Lewis*. Wheaton, IL: Harold Shaw, 1978.

Klapwijk, Jacob. *Purpose in the Living World? Creation and Emergent Evolution*. Cambridge: Cambridge University Press, 2008.

Knickerbocker, W. E. Jr. "The Myth That Saves: C. S. Lewis and the Doctrine of Theosis." *Touchstone: A Journal of Mere Christianity* 13/6 (2000). www.touchstonemag.com.

Kreeft, Peter. *Between Heaven and Hell: A Dialog Somewhere beyond Death with John F. Kennedy, C. S. Lewis and Aldous Huxley*. Downers Grove, IL: InterVarsity, 1982.

Kripke, Saul. "Naming and Necessity." In *The Semantics of Natural Languages*, edited by Donald Davidson and Gilbert Harman, 253–355. Dordrecht and Boston: Reidel, 1972.

Lampe, Geoffrey W. H. *A Patristic Greek Lexicon*. Oxford: Clarendon, 1961.

Lee, Matthew. "To Reign in Hell or to Serve in Heaven: C. S. Lewis on the Problem of Hell and the Enjoyment of the Good." In *C. S. Lewis as Philosopher: Truth, Goodness,*

BIBLIOGRAPHY

and Beauty, edited by David Baggett et al, 159-74. Downers Grove, IL: InterVarsity Press, 2008.

Leibniz, Gottfried W. "The Monadology." In Gottfried Wilhelm Leibniz, *Philosophical Papers and Letters,* edited by Leroy E. Loemker, 643-53. Dordrecht: D. Reidel, 1969.

Linzey, Andrew. *Animal Theology.* Chapagne, IL: Illinois University Press, 1995.

———. "C. S. Lewis' Theology of Animals." *Anglican Theological Review* 80/1 (1998): 60-82.

Lloyd, M. "Fall." *The Dictionary of Ethics, Theology and Society,* edited by Paul Barry Clarke and Andrew Linzey, 368-70. London: Routledge, 1996.

Lossky, Vladimir. *The Mystical Theology of the Eastern Church.* Crestwood, NY: St. Vladimir's Seminary Press, 1998.

Lovelock, J. *Gaia: A New Look at Life on Earth.* Oxford: Oxford University Press, 1979.

McCormack, Bruce L. "For Us and Our Salvation: Incarnation and Atonement in the Reformed Tradition." *Greek Orthodox Theological Review* 43 (1998): 281-316.

McCormack, Bruce L. "What's at Stake in Current Debates over Justification? The Crisis of Protestantism in the West." In *Justification: What's at Stake in the Current Debates,* edited by M. Husbands and D. J. Treier, 81-117. Downers Grove, IL: IVP Academic, 2004.

———. "Participation in God, Yes, Deification, No: Two Modern Protestant Responses to an Ancient Question." In *Denkwürdiges Geheimnis: Beiträge zur Gotteslehre. Festschrift für Eberhard Jüngel zum 70. Geburtstag.* Edited by I. U. Dalferth, J. Fischer, and H-P. Großhans, 347-74. Tübingen: Mohr-Siebeck, 2004.

McCracken, B. "Foundations Mission Impacts the Life of UCLA Grad Student." *The Chronicles of the C. S. Lewis Foundation* (Autumn/Winter 2007), 1. Online: www.cslewisclassics.com.

McGrath, Alister E. *The Intellectual World of C. S. Lewis.* Malden, MA: Wiley-Blackwell, 2013.

Mantzaridis, Georgios I. *The Deification of Man: St. Gregory Palamas and the Orthodox Tradition.* Translated by Liadain Sherrard. Crestwood, NY: St. Vladimir's Seminary Press, 1984.

Martel, Yann. *Life of Pi.* Orlando, FL: Harcourt, 2001.

Martindale, Wayne. *Beyond the Shadowlands: C. S. Lewis on Heaven and Hell.* Wheaton, IL: Crossway Books, 2005.

Mangina, Joseph. "Mediating Theologies: Karl Barth between Radical and Neo-orthodoxy." *Scottish Journal of Theology* 56/4 (2003): 427-43.

Meconi, David V. "Deification in the Thought of John Paul II." *Irish Theological Quarterly* 71 (2006): 127-41.

Meilander, Gilbert. *The Taste for the Other: The Social and Ethical Thought of C. S. Lewis.* Grand Rapids: Eerdmans, 1978.

Meyendorff, John. "Theosis in the Eastern Christian Tradition." In *Christian Spirituality II.* New York: Crossroad, 1989.

Mitchell, C. "Transposition in Relation to Narnia and Other Worlds: A Lecture." Lewis for Everyone Conference, Robert Menzies College, Macquarie University, Sydney, Australia, 6 May, 2006. Online: http://www.cslewistoday.com/files/mitchell-transposition.mp3.

Moorman, Charles. *Precincts of Felicity.* Tallahassee: University of Florida Press, 1966.

Morriston, Wes. "What if God Commanded Something Terrible? A Worry for Divine-command Meta-ethics." *Religious Studies* 45 (2009): 249-67.

---. "God and the Ontological Foundation of Morality." *Religious Studies* 48 (2011): 15–34.
Mosser, Carl. "The Earliest Patristic Interpretations of Psalm 82, Jewish Antecedents, and the Origin of Christian Deification." *Journal of Theological Studies* 56 (2005): 30–74.
Murphy, Gannon. "Reformed Theosis?" *Theology Today* 65 (2008): 191–212.
Murphy, Mark. "Theological Voluntarism." *Stanford Encyclopedia of Philosophy*. Online: http://plato.stanford.edu/entries/voluntarism-theological/.
---. "Theism, Atheism and the Explanation of Moral Value." In *Is Goodness without God Good Enough? A Debate on Faith Secularism and Ethics*, edited by Robert K. Garcia and Nathan King, 117–32. Lanham, MD: Rowman and Littlefield, 2009.
Myers, Doris T. *Bareface: A Guide to C. S. Lewis's Last Novel*. Columbia: University of Missouri Press, 2004.
Nellas, Panayiotis. *Deification in Christ*. Translated by Norman Russell. Crestwood, NY: St Vladimir's Seminary Press, 1987.
Newey, Edmund. "The Form of Reason: Participation in the Work of Richard Hooker, Benjamin Wichcote, Ralph Cudworth and Jeremy Taylor." *Modern Theology* 18 (2002): 1–26.
Oakley, Francis, and Elliot W. Urdang. "Locke, Natural Law and God." *Natural Law Forum* 11 (1966): 92–109.
Packer, James I. "What Lewis Was and Wasn't." *Christianity Today* 32/1 (January 1988): 11.
Otto, Randall E. "The Use and Abuse of Perichoresis in Recent Theology." *Scottish Journal of Theology* 54 (2001): 366–84.
Paley, William. *The Principles of Moral and Political Philosophy*. Indianapolis: Liberty Fund, 2002.
Passantino, G. "Are We Destined to Be Gods and Goddesses?: Does C. S. Lewis Defend Mormonism's 'Progression to Godhood?'" *Cornerstone Magazine* 29 (2000), at www.cornerstonemag.com.
Peterson, E. H. *Take and Read*. Grand Rapids: Eerdmans, 1996.
---. *A Long Obedience in the Same Direction*. Downers Grove, IL: InterVarsity Press, 2000.
Pearce, Joseph. *C. S. Lewis and the Catholic Church*. San Francisco: Ignatius Press, 2003.
Plantinga, Alvin. "Does God Have a Nature?" In *The Analytic Thiest: An Alvin Plantinga Reader*, edited by James F. Sennett, 226–56. Grand Rapids: Eerdmans, 1998.
---. "Naturalism, Theism, Obligation and Supervenience." Available at http://www.ammonius.org/grant_topics.php#0708.
Plantinga, Alvin. *Warrant and Proper Function*. New York: Oxford University Press, 1993.
Pascal, Blaise. *Pensées*. Edited by William Benton. Chicago: Regnery, 1952.
Perl, E. "The Presence of the Paradigm: Immanence and Transcendence in Plato's Theory of Forms." *The Review of Metaphysics* 53/2 (Dec 1999).
Putnam, Hilary. "The Meaning of Meaning." In *Mind, Language and Reality: Philosophical Papers*, 2:215–75. Cambridge: Cambridge University Press, 1975.
Polanyi, Michael. *Personal Knowledge: Towards a Post-critical Philosophy*. Chicago: University of Chicago Press, 1962.
Quinn, Philip. "An Argument for Divine Command Theory." In *Christian Theism and the Problems of Philosophy*, edited by Michael Beaty, 291. Notre Dame, IN: University of Notre Dame Press, 1990.
Ramsey, William. "Naturalism Defended." In *Naturalism Defeated?*, 15–29. Ithaca: Cornell University Press, 2002.

Reppert, Victor. *C. S. Lewis's Dangerous Idea: A Philosophical Defense of Lewis's Argument from Reason*. Downers Grove, IL: InterVarsity Press, 2003.
Richie, T. "Transposition and Tongues: Pentecostalizing an Important Insight of C. S. Lewis." *Journal of Pentecostal Theology* 13 (2004): 117–37.
Robinson, M. *Absence of Mind*. New Haven: Yale University Press, 2011.
Russell, N. *The Doctrine of Deification in the Greek Patristic Tradition*. Oxford: Oxford University Press, 2004.
Sapp, J. *Genesis: The Evolution of Biology*. Oxford: Oxford University Press, 2003.
Sayer, George. *Jack: A Life of C. S. Lewis*. Wheaton: Crossway Books, 1988.
Schakel, Peter J. "Till We Have Faces." In *The Cambridge Companion to C. S. Lewis*, ed. Robert MacSwain and Michael Ward, 281–93. Cambridge: Cambridge University Press, 2010.
Sheldrake, R. *Morphic Resonance: The Nature of Formative Causation*. South Paris, ME: Park Street Press, 2009.
Shun, Kwong-loi. "Confucianism" and "Taoism." In *The Oxford Companion to Philosophy*, ed. Ted Honderich. New York: Oxford University Press, 1995.
Slater, Jonathan. "Salvation as Participation in the Humanity of the Mediator in Calvin's *Institutes of the Christian Religion*: A Reply to Carl Mosser." *Scottish Journal of Theology* 58 (2005): 39–58.
Southgate, C. *The Groaning of Creation: Evolution and the Problem of Evil*. Louisville: Westminster/John Knox, 2009.
Stavropoulos, Christoforos. *Partakers of the Divine Nature*. Minneapolis: Light and Life, 1976.
Stephenson, Evan. "The Last Battle: C. S. Lewis and Mormonism." *Dialog* 30/4 (1997): 51.
Tolkien, J. R. R. *Tree and Leaf (Including the Poem "Mythopoeia")*. London: Grafton, 1992.
Tooley, Michael. "Opening Statement." A Classic Debate on the Existence of God: A Debate between Michael Tooley and William Lane Craig, University of Colorado at Boulder, November 1994. Transcript available at http://www.reasonablefaith.org/site/News2?page=NewsArticle&id=5307#section_3 ac.
———. "Does God Exist?" In *Knowledge of God*, ed. Alvin Plantinga and Michael Tooley, 70–150. Malden, MA: Blackwell, 2008.
Torrance, T. F. *Karl Barth: Biblical and Evangelical Theologian*. Edinburgh: T&T Clark, 1990.
———. *Divine Contingent Reality*. Oxford: Oxford University Press, 1981.
———. *Christian Theology and Scientific Culture*. New York: Oxford University Press, 1981.
Underhill, E. *The Letters of Evelyn Underhill*. Edited by C. Williams. London: Longmans, Green & Co., 1943.
Van Inwagen, Peter. *The Problem of Evil*. New York: Oxford University Press, 2006.
Van Leeuwen, M. S. "A Sword between the Sexes: C. S. Lewis's Long Journey to Gender Equality." *Christian Scholar's Review* 36/4 (Summer 2007): 391.
———. "What Did C. S. Lewis Say, and When Did He Say It? A Reply to Adam Barkman." *Christian Scholar's Review* 36/4 (Summer 2007): 437.
Wainwright, William. *Religion and Morality*. Aldershot: Ashgate, 2005.
Walker, A. "Scripture, Revelation and Platonism in C. S. Lewis." *Scottish Journal of Theology* 55/1 (2002): 19–35.
Ward, Michael. *Planet Narnia: Seven Heavens in the Imagination of C. S. Lewis*. Oxford: Oxford University Press, 2008.

Webb, Stephen H. "Aslan's Voice: C. S. Lewis and the Magic of Sound." In *The Chronicles of Narnia and Philosophy: The Lion the Witch and the Worldview*, ed. G. Bassham and J. L. Walls. Peru, IL: Carus, 2005.

Weirenga, Edward. *The Nature of God: An Inquiry into the Divine Attributes*. Ithaca, NY: Cornell University Press, 1989.

———. "Utilitarianism and the Divine Command Theory." *American Philosophical Quarterly* 21 (1984): 311–18.

———. "A Defensible Divine Command Theory." *Nous* 17 (1983): 387–408.

Wilson, A. N. *C. S. Lewis: A Biography*. London: Collins, 1990.

Wolfe, Judith. "C. S. Lewis and the Eschatological Church." In *C. S. Lewis and the Church: Essays in Honour of Walter Hooper*, ed. Judith Wolfe and Brendan N. Wolfe, 103–16. London: T&T Clark, 2011.

Wood, Ralph C. "Conflict and Convergence on Fundamental Matters in C. S. Lewis and J. R. R. Tolkien." *Renascence: Essays on Values in Literature* 55 (2003).

www.ingramcontent.com/pod-product-compliance
Lightning Source LLC
Chambersburg PA
CBHW051950160426
43198CB00013B/2378